SOBERTUDE

50 UPLIFTING HABITS
THAT CREATE GRATITUDE,
ABUNDANCE AND JOY IN SOBRIETY
(An Action Plan Guide)

By
DIRK FOSTER

Connect With Me:

I HAVE A FREE GIFT FOR YOU: Join My Newsletter and Receive a FREE BOOK at *www.thesoberjourney.com*

Facebook: *www.facebook.com/sobertravels/*

Author Page: *https://www.facebook.com/Dirk-Foster-Author-105017227522728/?modal=admin_todo_tour*

Other Books by Dirk Foster:

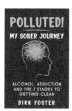 **Polluted: My Sober Journey: Alcohol, Addiction and The 7 Stages to Getting Clean**

 **The Sober Journey: A Guide to Prayer and Meditation in Recovery**

 **Sober Body: A Guide to Health and Fitness in Sobriety**

 **Sober and Broke: How to Make Money, Save Money, Pay Debt and Find Financial Peace is Sobriety**

TABLE OF CONTENT

SOBERTUDE

WHAT IS SOBERTUDE?

Getting sober is never easy. Staying sober is often just as difficult. Giving up alcohol (or drugs) is a great achievement for anyone. If you've managed to get sober, or are currently trying to get sober, congratulations! You've made a great decision that will improve your life and the lives of the people you love. Stick with it and never give up; it's worth the effort.

However, it's important to remember that once we get sober and manage to put away the destructive substances that were harming us, we still have to face life in all of its chaos. There will be daily challenges, turmoil, and difficulties for all of us, no matter how long we've been sober. Just because we get sober doesn't mean the rest of our days on earth are going to be simple and care-free, without disturbances, sadness, or pain. Sorrow and suffering are a part of experiencing a full life, just as much as joy and pleasure. **But naturally, we want to experience more abundance, happiness, and positivity than sadness and pain; and that's what this book attempts to provide.**

To fully experience all the positivity and abundance that sobriety (and life) can offer, you must cultivate a positive attitude – every day! That's what "Sobertude" means, *developing a positive attitude-of-gratitude in sobriety.*

- **Sobertude means taking daily action to improve your state of mind.**

- **Sobertude means developing optimism and rejecting pessimism.**

- **Sobertude means creating joy instead of sadness.**

- **Sobertude means proactively lifting your mood and spirit.**

- **Sobertude means cultivating happiness instead of anger.**

- **Sobertude means contributing positivity to the world.**

- **Sobertude means seeing the best in others.**

- **Sobertude means counting your blessings every day.**

- **Sobertude means accepting your character defects with humor.**

- **Sobertude means replacing self-pity with gratitude.**

It's not enough to simply stop drinking then waiting passively for life to bloom into perfection instantaneously. It doesn't work that way. Instead, you have to take proactive action, cultivating a positive and productive outlook. **You have to work on how you feel on the inside so that you can manifest what you want on the outside.** Once you do that, it's incredible how quickly every part of your life will begin to improve. Once you start to develop a positive "sobertude," other people will want to spend more time with you, you will experience greater abundance in every part of your life, and you will achieve more serenity and joy.

HOW THIS BOOK CAN HELP YOU

We can all use an attitude adjustment from time to time. That includes me. I've been sober for a long time (over 12 years as of this writing), but I still have to keep a positive attitude every day. My default modes, like that of many alcoholics and addicts, are pessimism, sullenness, and self-pity. I often wake up in a foul mood, and if I'm not careful, I'll carry that poor attitude into my entire day. My "stinking-thinking" will pollute not only my day but can also negatively impact my wife's day as well as that of friends and even strangers. *Beware the poor soul who crosses the path of a recovering addict in a foul mood.*

Resentment. Self-Pity. Anger. These are some of the most common traits of recovering alcoholics and addicts. We carry a lot of emotional baggage, often developed over many years of addiction. We often see the glass half-empty instead of <u>choosing</u> to see it as half-full. How we see the world is a matter of choice. **We can either be angry or happy; it all depends on the actions we take and the choices we make each day.**

- **Do you want to be happy? Then choose to be happy.**

- **Do you want to feel good about yourself? Then choose to feel good about yourself.**

- **Do you want to surround yourself with friendly people and beautiful things? Then choose nice people as friends and find beauty wherever you look.**

- **Do you want to be successful in life? Then choose to be successful in everything you want to achieve.**

Happiness, peace, and joy are all within reach to anyone willing to take the right steps by developing simple habits to improve their attitude and outlook on life.

In my opinion, Steve Martin, one of the greatest comedians of all time, once quipped, *"Before I go out, I put a slice of bologna in each of my shoes. So when I'm on stage, I feel funny."*

It's unlikely that Mr. Martin was serious when he said this. Still, it demonstrates the point of this book, and it is worth noting that *we usually have to take some kind of action, no matter how silly or odd it might seem, to change the way we feel and to move our attitude in a positive direction.*

Practicing the **50 Sobertude Habits** included in this book is similar to adding drops of clean water into a glass filled with dirty water. Eventually, drop by drop, the clean water will replace the dirty water until only clear, nourishing water to is there to drink.

This is how you have to attend to your attitude in sobriety; drop by drop, habit by habit, replacing your negative, polluted thinking and actions with clear, clean thoughts and actions. Once you develop these habits on a daily basis, the world will become a more beautiful and friendly place to explore and enjoy. You will experience more happiness and success once you learn to cultivate an attitude-of-gratitude.

THE BENEFITS OF SOBERTUDE

Extensive scientific and anecdotal research has proven that a positive attitude is crucial to good health, success, and long life. You don't have to be a genius to recognize that positive people are also fun to be around. No one wants to spend time with a Debbie-Downer or Angry-Andy whose outlook on life is always downbeat and negative. Life is too short to spend our precious time around people who are always whining, grumbling, and complaining.

And none of us WANTS TO BE THAT PERSON, either. Have you ever known someone who is so relentlessly negative that being in their presence is depressing? Don't be that person. Instead, try to be the person who lights up a room when you enter, the kind of person people WANT to be around because you make them feel happy.

The positive people, the upbeat and optimistic ones, are the ones who seem to bring happiness, laughter, and joy wherever they go. Those are the people we all want to be around and to emulate.

A positive attitude has a multitude of benefits to both your mental and physical health and well-being, including:

- **Better social life**
- **Improved romantic life**
- **Decreased stress**
- **Increased immunity**

- Lower blood pressure
- Longer life-span
- Less depression
- Reduced anxiety
- Better coping skills
- Improved psychological well-being
- Better digestion
- Improved appetite
- Reduced migraines
- Improved emotional fitness
- Increased sense of humor

Most importantly, as a recovering alcoholic or addict, **developing a positive attitude will create a powerful barrier between you and relapse**. Think of "sobertude" as a deep, wide moat surrounding your castle of sobriety. Keep the moat filled with the clean, clear water of positivity, and the armies of negativity that threaten your recovery will be unable to cross the divide and attack you.

HOW TO USE THIS BOOK

As the saying goes, *keep things simple.* To get the most benefit from this book, simply read one or two Sobertudes each day. Then follow the simple Action Plan to the best of your abilities.

- If you prefer, read the entire book all the way through; but you'll probably find it most helpful to practice just one or two Sobertudes per day.

- The idea is to plant the seed of positivity suggested by each Sobertude, so you have it in your head for the rest of the day.

- After reading each Sobertude, implement it into your life quickly, preferably the same day whenever possible.

- Meditate on it. Share it with a friend. Write about it in a journal or this book, or discuss it on social media.

- If you find one that doesn't suit you or feels uncomfortable for some reason, discard it and move on to the next one. There isn't going to be a test at the end, so relax and simply enjoy the journey of self-discovery.

Over time, many of these new habits will become second nature as you practice them. What's important is that you **take a proactive approach** to this adventure. This is an opportunity to learn about your mind and to improve your behavior, outlook, and optimism. This will be an excellent way for you to grow while protecting your sobriety at the same time.

So smile and let's get started.

SOBERTUDE HABIT #1 — CULTIVATE GRATITUDE

Gratitude is by far the most important thing to cultivate in your life. Gratitude is like a garden, which, if tended to every day, will produce beautiful results. Gratitude is a positive energy source that will deliver strength, courage, and joy, no matter what challenges you face.

If you're anything like me, your life has included many highs and many lows. As a recovering alcoholic and addict, I can assure you that I have experienced a great deal of pain and suffering and have battled a multitude of inner-demons over the years. To this day, I struggle with self-doubt, depression, grief, and sadness. Like every other person on earth, alcoholic or not, I have to work at finding happiness, joy, and peace. One of the ways I do this is by cultivating gratitude, no matter what life might throw at me.

Gratitude is the conscious act of feeling thankful for your blessings. This doesn't mean you ignore the difficulties in your path or act like pain and suffering don't exist. Instead, you counteract suffering by recognizing that no matter how bad things might be at the moment, there are always things to be thankful for in your life.

How do we begin to focus on gratitude if we don't necessarily feel gratitude or don't know where to find it? Simple; **start with where you are right now**!

Look around you, and I guarantee you'll find something that you can appreciate. It can be anything. Perhaps it's the fact that you have a healthy body that still works and a roof over your head. Or maybe you have something delicious in your kitchen that you can eat, or there's a good television show tonight that you enjoy. If you try hard enough, you will always be able to find at least one or two things to be grateful about: a favorite pet; a good meal; a soft pillow to sleep on; a song you love; a joke that makes you laugh; a good cup of coffee. Be on the lookout for the things in life that bring you joy, no matter how fleeting or insignificant they might seem.

Start with the simple things. Don't focus on the negatives; focus only on things that make you smile and bring you joy.

Over time, expand your list to other areas of your life that make you feel grateful. Perhaps a person you met or the people you love, or an interesting conversation you had, or a work of art you admire. By cultivating gratitude in your daily life, you're much more likely to discover acceptance, peace, and serenity, the ultimate goal of living.

Gratitude should be your number one goal (that's why it's the first on our list). By cultivating a deep sense of gratitude for the good things rather than focusing on the negatives, your garden of joy and happiness will bloom as you absorb the sunlight of thankfulness.

ACTION PLAN

List 3 things that you are grateful for in your life. Keep it simple as you start. Perhaps it's the roof over your head, the food in your refrigerator, or a favorite song. Write any three things that come to your mind that make you feel happy, safe, or content. Try doing this every morning, either mentally or by writing it down.

SOBERTUDE

Today I'm grateful for the following:

1.

2.

3.

SOBERTUDE HABIT #2 — SET (REALISTIC) GOALS

Imagine you have to take a trip across the United States to attend a friend's wedding. You live in California, and the wedding is in Maine. This means you have to traverse the entire country to get there, but you're afraid of flying, so you choose to drive instead. The problem is that you've never driven across the country. You don't know how long the drive will take or how much gasoline you'll need. And you don't know which roads and highways will lead you in the right direction.

Essentially, you don't have the foggiest idea of how to get to the wedding. So now what?

You have two options: **Option 1**) Start driving without a clear plan, crisscrossing the country while praying you'll find your way to the wedding before you die of old age. **Option 2**) Develop a plan using a map, a budget, and a schedule to ensure you arrive at your friend's wedding on time. Obviously, option 2 is the wisest choice.

Setting realistic goals is essential to obtaining the things you want in life, just like planning a cross-country road trip requires a map, a schedule, and a budget.

Too often we decide we want something, but never create a clear plan about getting it. Simply deciding we want something without setting up realistic goals to obtain it is like driving blindly around the country, *hoping and praying* to find where you want to go. Most likely, you're just going to end up driving in circles without ever reaching your destination.

The top reasons to set goals:

- Goals give you focus and a clear vision.
- Goals allow you to measure progress.
- Goals encourage you to take action.
- Goals give you motivation.
- Goals make it more likely you'll obtain what you want.
- Goals help you organize your time and actions.

Are there certain things you want out of life? Are there things you've always wanted to achieve, learn, or experience? Perhaps you want to start a new career or travel to an exotic country. Maybe you want to write a book, learn how to play guitar or launch your own company. Whatever you dream of having or doing, set up a clear set of goals you can follow, like a map leading you to your destination.

It's also essential to keep your goals *realistic*. There's no sense in deciding you want to become an astronaut and fly to the moon if you're 70 years old, blind, and have a heart condition. NASA probably won't be interested in your services. Instead, set goals that are in-line with your circumstances and abilities. Keep things simple as you start, and over time you can add more dreams and goals to your life that are increasingly challenging but also realistic.

ACTION PLAN

List two goals that you want to achieve over the next week. Keep them realistic and straightforward. Perhaps you want to exercise more often or update your resume. Whatever your goals are, make sure they are within the realm of possibility for your given circumstances.

Goal #1:

Goal #2:

List 3 steps you will take to achieve each goal:

Goal # 1 Steps

Step 1:

Step 2:

Step 3:

Goal #2 Steps

Step 1:

Step 2:

Step 3:

SOBERTUDE HABIT #3 — LEARN MEDITATION

The mind of a typical addict is like a wild animal trapped in a cage. It needs to be trained appropriately to calm the animal so that it can find peace and comfort. Meditation is the best form of mental training for most alcoholics and addicts, an easy and enjoyable technique to help soothe the savage beast trapped in our heads.

While various cultures around the world have developed many forms of meditation, Buddhist meditation is arguably the most widely recognized and practiced. The easiest way to describe Buddhist meditation is the practice of **emptying the mind.**

The phrase "emptying the mind" sounds a lot like "taking out the trash" or "cleaning out the garage." And in a way, they're very similar. When you attempt to empty your mind, you're trying to clear away the dark debris of suffering, pain, regret, and angst that plague your conscious and subconscious life. Your mind is a lot like a garage filled with junk that has accumulated over many years. You know the garage needs cleaning, but you keep putting it off as long as possible. Then one day, you turn on the light and are confronted by a mountain of rubbish. Sooner or later, you have to empty the garage, or the problem will keep getting worse.

One of the great things about meditation is that it lets you first **recognize your source of suffering**. If you're able to see what is causing the pain (*negative thoughts*), you can release it with a smile. You can train your mind (*the wild beast*) to release the negative thoughts that hold you hostage. Empty your mind of destructive thoughts and cravings, and your mind will fill with peace and acceptance.

A helpful image to illustrate the point is a helium balloon released into the sky. Once you have identified a negative thought, instead of holding onto it, think of it as a red balloon that you want to release. Let it go and watch as it drifts upwards into the clouds, finally disappearing out of sight. Perhaps it sounds simplistic, but it works.

There are times when negative thoughts are buried so deep and are so painful, that we need to seek professional help to dislodge them. But meditation can help you explore the inner workings of your mind so that you can begin letting go of the harmful debris you've been hoarding.

The simplest way to meditate is to **sit comfortably** in a chair or on a couch (legs crossed or not, it's up to you), close your eyes and **focus on your breath**. Breathe naturally through your nostrils. You don't need to pant or exaggerate each breath, just follow the normal flow of air as it passes in and out of your nose. Feel your chest and shoulders gently rise and fall with each breath. As thoughts come into your mind, push them aside, then bring your attention back to your breath. **Focus only on your breathing.** It's as simple as that.

Meditation doesn't need to be complicated. If you're entirely new to it, you can just try it for 2-3 minutes. Then you can try it twice per day. As you get used to it, increase the amount of time you meditate to 5 minutes. Eventually, you'll find it easier and easier to sit for long periods without even noticing.

ACTION PLAN

Pick a time to meditate each day. Mornings might be the best time since this is a time when most people are at their grumpiest,

21

therefore the most pessimistic. Pick a comfortable place to sit, close your eyes, and focus on breathing for a few minutes. Over time, add a few more minutes to each session and try meditating twice per day, once in the morning and once at night. Take note of the **time you start** each day and **how many minutes** you're able to sit comfortably with your eyes shut.

Most importantly, don't stress out if it feels like you're doing it wrong. There's no perfect way to meditate. Just do your best.

Day 1: Time of Day: **Number of Minutes:**

Day 2: Time of Day: **Number of Minutes:**

Day 3: Time of Day: **Number of Minutes:**

Day 4: Time of Day: **Number of Minutes:**

Day 5: Time of Day: **Number of Minutes:**

SOBERTUDE HABIT #4 —
FORGIVE OTHERS (AND YOURSELF)

Have you been harmed by others? Have you hurt other people? Have you inflicted harm on yourself? If you've been alive on earth for more than ten minutes, the most likely answer to each of these questions is a definite, YES!

- If others have harmed you, you probably carry *resentment*.

- If you've hurt others, you probably carry *guilt*.

- If you've hurt yourself, you probably carry *shame*.

Resentment, guilt, and shame are destructive emotions that inflict long-term damage to your heart, mind, and soul. Just like you have to rid yourself of negative thinking, you also have to cleanse yourself of the psychological poisons of resentment, guilt, and shame. **Forgiveness** is the only way to get clean finally.

Practicing forgiveness is not an easy thing to do, especially if you feel you've been grievously harmed. We live in a culture that often glorifies and promotes vengeance and retaliation. Hollywood churns out an endless barrage of movies every year that romanticizes revenge and blood-lust. Pop songs are filled with fantasies of "getting back" at perceived slights and broken hearts. Politicians build careers out of exacting revenge from their opponents. The news media encourages division amongst various factions in society just to increase their ratings and sell commercials.

SOBERTUDE

No wonder we find it so difficult to forgive; we're constantly inundated with the notion that revenge is a justified means-to-an-end which will bring us some form of dubious satisfaction.

In reality, resentment and revenge usually just create more pain and suffering for everyone involved. If we're unable to forgive others, we will remain in a perpetual state of misery and anger. If we're unable to forgive ourselves, we will stay in a constant state of shame and regret.

The easiest way to begin the process of forgiveness is to write down the name of whoever hurt you on a piece of paper. Then list what they did that caused you harm. After that, describe how you were hurt and how it affected your life. Finally, commit to forgiving them – every day, if necessary – to release your anger into the wind.

It might not be easy when you first start, but eventually, the benefits you reap, and the relief you feel will far outweigh the difficulty and effort it requires.

ACTION PLAN

Complete forgiveness probably won't happen immediately in most cases. But if you make it a point to keep forgiving each person every day, slowly but surely, your resentment and anger will begin to dissolve. For each person that has hurt you (including yourself) follow these steps:

- **Name each person who hurt you:**

- **Briefly, describe what each person did that hurt you (Example: "*Joe Smith cheated on me.*"):**

- **In a few words, describe how you were you effected by their action (Example: "*My sense of safety and trust were shattered.*"):**

SOBERTUDE HABIT #4 – FORGIVE OTHERS (AND YOURSELF)

- Forgive each person (Example: *"Today I have decided to forgive Joe Smith for cheating on me because I no longer wish to carry the pain it caused me in my heart any longer."*):

SOBERTUDE HABIT #5 — SEEK INSPIRATION

What makes you smile? What motivates you? Is there an activity, hobby, or subject that fills you with curiosity and joy? Have you ever wanted to learn an instrument or study art? Is there a particular type of music that warms your soul? Do you want to start your own business, write a book of poetry, or learn how to ballroom dance?

Everyone has something that makes them feel motivated and inspired, a topic or activity that excites their soul. For me, I always wanted to write a book. I spent decades *THINKING* about writing a book, but I never got around to *WRITING* a book because I was too afraid to face the possibility of failure. I procrastinated for years and years, never putting pen to paper.

Writing (and reading) was always the thing that inspired me the most. Even when I was a small boy, I harbored a dream of one day being a writer. I wasn't even sure what that meant, but it stuck with me for decades. Books, literature, and poetry became the driving force in my life (besides drinking) and always filled me with joy and a sense of purpose. I was obsessed with literary figures like F. Scott Fitzgerald, Ernest Hemingway, and Henry Miller.

It wasn't until I got sober and made some considerable changes in my life that I found the courage and *INSPIRATION* to finally begin writing in earnest. If you're reading this right now, this is the 5th book I've written.

What inspires you? What fills your soul with longing and desire?

Things that inspire you don't necessarily have anything to do with making money or earning a living. It's often the exact opposite. If you're inspired by reading Greek philosophy or Shakespeare, it will be tough to extract an income from these pursuits (unless you're inspired to be a teacher). What matters the most is finding and pursuing things that motivate you, stimulate your mind, get your blood pumping, and fill you with excitement.

It doesn't matter how old you are or how young. And never allow fear or self-doubt to control your desire to pursue the things that inspire you. What matters the most is identifying what inspires you and going after it with passion.

Have you always wanted to learn how to play music? Then buy an inexpensive guitar and a book of chords. Want to learn how to cook gourmet food? Go online and watch videos from professional chefs. Want to write a book of poetry? Take out a pen and start writing.

Whatever it is that inspires you, don't wait for it to show up on your doorstep "someday." Seek inspiration and pursue the things that excite you and move your soul.

ACTION PLAN

We often discard our passions in life as being trivial or childish because they seem impractical or don't generate money. Don't fall into that trap. Let your ideas and dreams soar, regardless of financial concerns. Identify a topic, interest, or hobby that brings you joy and inspires you and launch a plan to make it a reality in your life.

Write down one topic, interest or hobby you have always wanted to pursue (Example: "*I want to write a book.*"):

Create a simple plan to get started (Example: "*Today I will begin to outline my first novel.*"):

SOBERTUDE

Develop a simple schedule to follow (Example: *"I will spend 1 hour each evening working on my novel until the first draft is finished."*)**:**

SOBERTUDE HABIT #6 — SEEK OUT POSITIVE PEOPLE

Just like anger breeds anger, positivity breeds positivity. If you spend your time constantly surrounded by people who are always angry, bitter, and cynical, guess what? You're going to end up adopting those characteristics yourself.

Human beings are very adaptable creatures. Throughout our evolution on earth, we have learned to absorb and emulate certain traits and characteristics of other humans in our proximity. This isn't necessarily a bad thing. It's a survival technique that allows groups of people to act as a singular unit, or tribe, to ward off outside dangers and threats. The more we think alike, the more prepared we'll be to fight off danger as a singular entity. It's similar to the way the military trains recruits; *individual thought* must be replaced by *group thought* to maximize efficiency and strength.

But this group mentality will also produce negative results for you as an individual if you're not careful. If you spend too much time around cynics and doomsayers, you'll eventually be dragged down to their level. Instead of basking in the sunlight of optimism, you'll end up covered in the mud of pessimism.

Make it a point to surround yourself with people who lift you up with positive vibes rather than bring you down. Positive, optimistic people are the ones who encourage you and make you feel better about yourself. They look for ways to add humor, hope, and love into the world. They enjoy bringing out the best in themselves and other people. Positive people work hard and play hard, and they love to see others do well in life.

If you're new to sobriety, you'll often find that the most upbeat and perpetually joyful people are the ones who have been sober for many years (the "old-timers" in 12-step circles). They've managed to cleanse themselves of the bitterness and anger that once polluted their souls. Their spiritual cleansing has given them a new view on life, a way of seeing the world as both realistic and positive. They know first-hand that life is often challenging, but they have *chosen* a path that replaces anger with joy, darkness with light, and hatred with love. They always have a lot of good hair-raising stories to tell, and they tell their stories with humor and wisdom born of struggle and redemption.

Seek out the people who lift you up and make you smile. Find the ones who spread kindness everywhere they go. Avoid the ones who bring you down by encouraging you to feel sour, sad, or miserable. Most importantly, avoid people who try to discourage your sobriety and your efforts to improve your life. Plain and simple, if someone in your life isn't ENCOURAGING you, there's a good chance they might be DISCOURAGING you.

Surround yourself with positive people and reap the rewards of the sunlight they cast over your world.

ACTION PLAN

Are there people in your life who constantly seem angry and bitter? Are there some who seem to want to bring other people down with a constant barrage of negativity? There's no reason to be cruel or hurtful towards these types of people. You should feel sorry for them. However, there's also no reason to spend too much time around them either. Search for people who are upbeat and filled with joy and make it a point to reach out to them as a friend whenever the opportunity appears.

- **Can you identify people who bring you (or others) down with constant negativity?:**

- **Can you identify people who always seem to be happy and helpful to others?:**

- **What steps can you take to introduce yourself to one positive person this week?:**

SOBERTUDE HABIT #7 — LAUGH OUTLOUD

Want to find a new drug that is free, legal, and won't kill you? Try laughter. Laughter is the best drug you will ever experience. Best of all, it doesn't cost a dime and won't destroy your health, life, or family. And the supply never runs out.

A great deal of scientific research has shown that laughter has enormous health benefits. Best of all, laughing is just plain fun and will brighten the mood of even the grumpiest curmudgeon. What are some of the reasons to laugh more?

- Laughter relaxes your mind and body
- Laughter releases endorphins (the brains feel-good drug)
- Laughter helps your heart by increasing blood flow
- Laughter dissolves anger
- Laughter improves your mood
- Laughter lifts your spirit
- Laughter decreases stress
- Laughter cheers up people around you
- Laughter decreases social tension
- Laughter improves relationships

SOBERTUDE HABIT #7 — LAUGH OUTLOUD

- Laughter promotes bonding and friendship
- Laughter diffuses conflict

Try to laugh out loud at least once per day (preferably more). Look for the humor in the world, observe the insanity and silliness of life in all its odd and magnificent glory.

If you can't find a way to laugh out loud on your own, find things that make you smile. For me, old Mel Brooks movies (Young Frankenstein, in particular) or certain TV shows (The Office) usually does the trick. My wife is a big fan of I Love Lucy, which seems to make her laugh consistently. You can also find a million funny videos on YouTube.

Whatever it is that makes you laugh, make it a point to laugh out loud every day. This will not only brighten up your day but will also cheer up those around you. Of course, we all have those days when nothing in the world is going to make us laugh no matter how hard we try. But usually, on most normal days, you can find a little humor somewhere that will lift your spirits.

ACTION PLAN

Write down a list of things that always make you laugh – old movies, TV shows, stand-up comedians, cartoons, books, etc. Keep the list handy and make it a point to review it whenever you're feeling particularly grumpy, depressed, or angry. No matter how bad your day is going, try to take a short break and enjoy a few minutes with whatever makes you laugh the most.

- **Identify any TV shows, movies, books, etc. that make you laugh the easiest. Write them down and keep them handy.**

- **Whenever you're feeling angry or depressed, review your list and take a few moments out of your day to laugh.**

SOBERTUDE HABIT #8 – LEARN A NEW JOKE

Since you're going to make it a point to laugh every day, you should also make it a point to learn a new joke every day. Having a pocket full of jokes at the ready any time you need it, will keep you amused and brighten up other people's day.

Jokes don't have to be brilliant or even told well to make us laugh. Some of the worst jokes in the world are the ones that make us laugh the loudest just because they're so awful. I love corny, sixth-grade humor. A joke that makes an average 12-year-old laugh is perfect for me. Other people prefer more sophisticated humor. Not me! Barf jokes, poop and fart jokes, jokes about your momma, and knock-knock jokes are about as fancy as I get when it comes to humor.

Maybe you like long, drawn jokes that reveal a hilarious punch line at the end. Perhaps you prefer jokes that rely on irony or an unexpected twist. Jokes are a lot like pizza and sex; even when they're bad, they're still good. Whatever works for you, it's easy to find a million new jokes. A few reasons to learn some jokes, even if they suck:

- Jokes ease social tension.

- Jokes make people smile (no matter how bad they are).

- Jokes reduce anxiety and stress.

34

- Jokes are good for family relationships.

- Jokes are good for romantic relationships.

- Jokes encourage conversation (often about how bad the joke is)

- Jokes release endorphins in our brain.

- Jokes point out absurdities in life.

- Jokes help us laugh with others.

- Jokes improve social bonding.

There's no magic trick when it comes to collecting new jokes. There are dozens of books you can buy online and countless videos you can watch that will provide you with an enormous amount of material or teach you how to write jokes.

And don't be shy about telling a joke, even to a perfect stranger. People are always looking for an excuse to laugh. Sometimes, a simple, silly joke will brighten up another person's day and cheer you up, too. Even the most poorly told joke can have a humorous impact on those around you.

ACTION PLAN

Try to learn a new joke every day. Buy a book of jokes or find a list of them online. Watch YouTube videos on timing and pacing. The jokes can be long or short, whichever is easiest for you to commit to memory. Repeat the joke several times to yourself, then try it out on a few friends or family members (a.k.a "victims"). And remember not to take yourself too seriously as you practice new jokes. At the very least, they'll get a good laugh at how badly you told the joke in the first place.

SOBERTUDE HABIT #9 — LEARN A NEW HOBBY

There are times when doing silly, or even stupid, activities is the best way to improve our mood and lift our spirit. It's easy to become so consumed by work and responsibilities that we forget to have fun. Sometimes the most meaningless activities are the most enjoyable moments of the day.

Children are the masters of silly activities. Watch any kid, especially when they're on their own, and witness how many goofy and fun things they come up with to amuse themselves. Many of us need to relearn how to be childlike in our appreciation of the silly side of life, or we'll be in danger of turning into moody old coots who take life WAY TOO SERIOUSLY.

Life should be enjoyed, not merely tolerated. Make it a priority to find at least one (or more) hobby that serves no discernable purpose other than to amuse you. Have you ever wanted to learn how to juggle? Do you want to learn how to play the ukulele? Do you want to build model ships or cars?

Recently my wife and I began participating in an online painting course. The instructor guides us (and the other participants) through a series of steps that eventually produces a simple landscape painting. I can state without hesitation that I have no artistic talent (that's my wife's department), but the experience is always relaxing and amusing. Neither of us plans to make a living as an artist (a chimp could produce better art than I can), but that's not the point. It gives us an opportunity to do something that we enjoy and isn't the least serious or crucial to our existence. IT'S JUST FUN!

There are countless activities that you can learn:

- Juggling
- Riding a unicycle
- Playing harmonica
- Painting or drawing
- Mastering the yoyo (no, really)
- Stamp or coin collecting
- Bird watching (a classic)
- Model building
- Board games
- Magic or card tricks
- Creating Haiku's
- Photography
- Hiking
- Knitting
- Gardening
- Dancing

The list is almost endless. There are many fun, even silly, hobbies you can discover and try. Some are ideal for one person, while others are better suited for couples. The point is to find something that will make you smile, fill some time, and maybe even make you feel like a kid again.

ACTION PLAN

- **List any activity or hobby that you want to learn:**

- **What steps will you take to learn a new hobby (Example: "*Watch videos on YouTube that teach me how to juggle.*")**

- **How often will you engage in this new silly activity (every day, once per week, etc.):**

SOBERTUDE HABIT #10 – LOOK FOR BEAUTY

Look for beauty in the world, not only in obvious places but *every-where*. Even when it seems impossible, it's essential to train your mind to seek out beauty wherever it might reveal itself to your eyes. The image of a *rose growing out of a sidewalk* may be a cliché, but it perfectly illustrates the point and can be used as an example of what to look for in your search.

The famous architect Frank Lloyd Wright once said: *"If you foolishly ignore beauty, then you will soon find yourself without it. Your life will be impoverished. But if you invest in beauty, it will remain with you all the days of your life."*

Even the most mundane, boring places in the world can hold secret gems of beauty. The more you invest in seeking out beauty where others might miss it, the richer your life experience will become. Anyone can find beauty in nature. That's easy. But those who can find beauty in every corner of the world, whether in fields of lilies or fields of concrete, will find themselves in a much better state of mind.

Perhaps you live in a big city that's filled with pollution and grime. Then look to the sky. Look at the clouds or the way the sunlight plays on the window panes surrounding you, or the unique shadows cast off the buildings. When there's a storm, listen to the rain falling, one of the most beautiful sounds in the universe. As the storm passes, admire the scent of fresh, clean air (and, of course, look for the rainbow).

There are very few places or situations when you can't find some form of beauty to lift your spirit. Often, it's merely a matter of knowing where and how to look.

Turn it into a game. As you travel through your day, whether you're in the heart of a city, driving on the freeway, or sitting in your kitchen, look for anything that stands out from the ordinary. Look for the little details, colors, and textures of the landscape that surrounds you. Search for the small signs of life dancing around you and admire what you find. Look for beauty in the faces of other people, in the laughter of a child, or the playfulness of a dog. If you look hard enough and train yourself how to see beauty everywhere, you'll discover that the world is filled with many wondrous things to behold.

ACTION PLAN

The easiest way to become aware of the beauty that surrounds you is by turning it into a daily game. Simply make it a point to identify several things each day that you feel are beautiful and appealing to witness.

- **Write down three things that are in the room with you that might be considered unusual or beautiful (Example: "*The shadow that's being cast off a table lamp.*"):**

- **Look for three things every day that you consider interesting or beautiful, in your home or outside in the world.**

40

SOBERTUDE HABIT #11 — LEARN DOWNWARD DOG

If you've never attempted yoga, it's time to start. Yes, I know it looks difficult, awkward, and sort of goofy. But yoga is one of the best things you can do for your body and mind, and I recommend it to anyone. There are yoga classes for beginners in every community in the United States. Start with a "gentle" or "basic" yoga class, and you will be amazed at how good it feels. You can find an abundance of yoga lessons on YouTube if you can't find a class near you.

Once you've learned the basics and get passed any feelings of awkwardness, the flow of yoga is a great way to calm anxiety and stress. Yoga, in one form or another, has been around for thousands of years. It's become trendy in Western culture over the last few decades because of its spiritually restorative attributes. It's also an excellent form of exercise.

Best of all, it can calm your mind and ease tension in your body. If you can focus all your attention on each movement, pose, and breath, then your mind will quiet down. Many people find that after they've tried yoga a few times, they become addicted to how it makes them feel. For many, it becomes a lifelong habit with infinite benefits.

Yoga is also a great form of exercise and will improve your physical fitness. You don't have to be athletic or even in very good shape to begin a basic yoga routine. There are also "chair yoga" classes that allow you to sit comfortably in a chair while doing specific poses and stretches for people with physical challenges. Combined with its intrinsic meditative qualities, yoga is a smart choice for just about everyone.

ACTION PLAN

The best place to start is to look for a class being in your community, either at a gym or yoga studio. There are various levels of yoga, including some that are highly advanced and difficult. So keep it simple at first, starting with a beginner or basic class for a few weeks or months before moving forward into the more complex variations of yoga.

- **Are you willing to try yoga a few times? Circle one: YES/NO**

- **Is there a yoga class, or studio, near your home? YES/NO**

- **If there are no classes or studios near you, can you find many courses online? YES/NO**

- **Do you have a friend or family member who might want to try yoga with you? YES/NO**

- **Write down how many days each week you can practice yoga.**

SOBERTUDE HABIT #12 — WALK MORE

Does the word "exercise" fill you with dread? When you hear the term "working out," do you panic and start looking for the nearest escape route to freedom? The fact is, exercise doesn't have to be feared or avoided. Instead, it should be welcomed and embraced. Exercise doesn't have to be difficult, either. Some of the most effective forms of exercise are easy and enjoyable. The only thing you need to do is find an activity that you enjoy, and that elevates your heart rate and pushes your muscles a little at a time. Start simple and experiment with various forms of exercise, and before you know it, you'll start feeling much better, sleeping well and losing weight

Walking is the most accessible and most immediate exercise routine available to you. It's like having your own gym that's open twenty-four hours per day. And it's very effective, too. There's no reason why you shouldn't be walking every day.

You don't have to walk long distances, either. Just go outside and walk for 10 or 15 minutes in the morning or evening (or both)

Walking is great for your leg and back muscles. The system of movement your body engages in when you walk has a positive effect on your entire physical structure, including your arms, shoulders, heart, and lungs. It's also great for *relieving stress and anxiety*, which is beneficial to your *mental and spiritual health.*

If you can walk somewhere instead of driving, then you should walk. If you need to go to the store and its close enough, walk there. If you have a friend who is elderly or lonely, be of service by asking if they want to take a short walk. If you have children, take them for a walk as an excuse to spend time with them. If you have a dog, take her for a long walk every day. If you have a cat, you can try putting a harness on him and take him for a walk (*but please don't blame me if people laugh at you*).

Walking is easy and enjoyable and will help you get into decent shape quickly. It's also an excellent way to clear your head, collect your thoughts, and diminish stress and anxiety. Don't wait for a perfect day or time or perfect weather (walking in the rain and snow is its own form of pleasure). Get started today. *And if you decide to take your cat for a walk, please take a photograph and send it to me. I can always use a good laugh.*

ACTION PLAN

Create a simple plan to start walking every day or every other day. Start with only 10 minutes if that seems like enough, but plan to work your way up to a daily 30-minute walk over time. Bring some music with you, or walk with a friend or pet.

- **Every day this week, I plan to walk _____ minutes per day.**

- **Every day next week, I plan to walk _____ minutes per day.**

SOBERTUDE HABIT #13 — EAT HEALTHY FOOD (DUH!)

As the saying goes, *you are what you eat*. What you put into your body every day has an immediate impact on every aspect of your physical and mental health. Good food is a gift. If you can learn how to appreciate food not only for how it tastes but also how it sustains you, you will be more likely to make wise choices every time you eat.

Your body is a natural engine that requires a constant input of fuel to run efficiently over a long time (many, many years, hopefully). So you must fill your body-engine with only the best fuel possible. Respect your body, and your body will show you respect. It's as simple as that.

Along with exercise and healthy body weight, natural, healthy foods are essential to staying fit and fighting disease. Certain foods reduce the risk of major health problems, including obesity, diabetes, heart disease and stroke, intestinal disorders like irritable bowel syndrome, all forms of cancer, immune disorders including lupus, certain eye diseases, chronic kidney disease, Alzheimer's disease, chronic pain syndromes, and asthma. The typical American diet that is high in fat and low in fiber is known to be a significant contributor to obesity, diabetes, and heart disease, mainly because they promote excess weight.

So, how can we avoid all these nasty illnesses? Look no further than your kitchen for powerful age and disease fighting foods that can keep you healthy and strong for many years.

While a plant-based diet is ideal, limiting the saturated fat content with non-dairy products and lean cuts of meat will help reduce the number of harmful components present in animal foods. You must avoid, as often as possible, junk food, high-fat meats, high-sugar foods, and fast food.

Eating healthy food doesn't always mean you have to deny yourself completely. You can still enjoy fun food, but in moderation. Just make it a habit to become more aware of what you're eating and keep a mental note by asking this question: *is this good for my body or bad for my body?* You will know the correct answer if you're honest with yourself. Two apples; good. Two pints of ice cream; bad.

You can even keep a note pad, or food journal, with you and write it down to help you remember. Try to develop a conscious awareness of what kind of foods you allow into your body. Do you tend to eat mostly processed or packaged food? Do you eat at fast-food restaurants every day? What are you drinking, sodas, or water? Do you eat fresh fruit every day?

10 Ideas for a healthier diet:

1. Add a fruit or vegetable to every meal.
2. Eat a handful of nuts daily.
3. Drink tea several times per day, especially green tea.
4. Eat legumes like kidney beans, split peas, and lentils three times per week.
5. Make all your grain choices whole-grain; brown rice, whole-wheat pasta, quinoa, buckwheat, etc.
6. Reduce the saturated fat content in recipes.

7. Squeeze the juice of a lemon or lime into your water, beverages or foods.

8. Go meatless three days per week (if you eat meat).

9. Sprinkle a tablespoon of ground flax or chia seed into salads, yogurt, and smoothies.

10. Increase the number of spices and herbs in your favorite recipes.

ACTION PLAN

Using a pad of paper, computer or smartphone, create a simple food journal that includes the day of the week and what you eat each day. Track your food every day, for at least four weeks, until you have a clear picture of what kind of food you eat and how often.

EXAMPLE

- **Day of the Week:** Monday

- **Time of Day:** 8:00 am **Type of Food Eaten:** Bowl of yogurt with fruit

- **Time of Day:** 10:00 am **Type of Food Eaten:** 1 hardboiled egg

- **Time of Day:** 12:00 pm **Type of Food Eaten:** Tuna sandwich on wheat bread

- **Time of Day:** 2:00 pm **Type of Food Eaten:** Green smoothie

- **Time of Day:** 6:00 pm **Type of Food Eaten:** Turkey burger with salad

- **Time of Day:** 7:00 pm **Type of Food Eaten:** Frozen yogurt

*Quick tip: Most nutritionists consider eating five small meals every day healthier than eating three large meals.

SOBERTUDE HABIT #14 — DRINK MORE WATER

One of the most important things (and easiest things) you can do to maintain your health is to keep a steady flow of water passing through your body. Every single cell in your body requires water to function properly. Your internal organs, skin, and hair all need an abundance of clean water.

Too often, many of us rely on sugary drinks and caffeinated beverages to get through the day. It's crucial to ingest more water than any other type of beverage to keep your system flushed, vibrant, and happy.

As you might have heard, up to 60% of the human body is made of water. Look at these statistics to get a clear understanding of the water content in an average adult body:

- The brain is composed of 73% water.
- The heart is composed of 73% water.
- The lungs are composed of 83% water.
- The skin is composed of 64% water.
- The muscles are composed of 79% water.
- The kidneys are composed of 79% water.
- The bones are composed of 31% water.

That's a lot of water we're carrying around! All that water, which is so essential to a high-functioning body, has to come from somewhere. Your muscles, in particular, need water to strengthen and grow. Every part of your body needs water to thrive. It's essential to keep the water flowing to keep your body going!

Keep water with you all the time. Not just when you're exercising. Carry a bottle with you to work, to the store, to school, every place you go. Keep water by your bedside. The more water you drink, the healthier you will look and feel.

ACTION PLAN

Health professionals often recommend the "8x8 rule", which suggests we drink 8 ounces of water eight times per day. Buy an eight-ounce drinking container and fill it eight times each day starting in the morning and ending an hour before bed.

SOBERTUDE HABIT #15 — EAT SUPERFOODS

In the simplest terms, superfoods are natural, nutrient-dense foods that supply your body with everything it needs to function at the highest level. For a food to be in the 'Super' category, it needs to be a power-hitter in the antioxidant and anti-inflammatory group, carrying the ability to protect your heart from damaging free radicals. High levels of free radicals cause inflammation and irritation in our arteries and vessels that cause heart attack and stroke. In addition to being high in antioxidants, vitamins, and minerals, Superfoods are good sources of fiber and can lower cholesterol.

Add these foods to your shopping list and experiment with them in your recipes and meals.

- **Green Leafy Vegetables** - By adding more veggies to your diet, you increase the volume of foods eaten while reducing calorie intake.

- **Apples** - The crunch in apples signals our brain that we're satisfied, and the natural sugars in fruit come loaded with fiber and antioxidants that make a perfect swap for processed sweets.

- **Nuts** - Nuts are healthy protein, healthy fat, and nutrient-packed to assist in eating less throughout the day. Keep to a 2-4 tablespoon portion, as nuts are caloric.

- **Beans and Legumes** - A great source of healthy carbs and proteins, they're high in fiber and slow down digestion, helping us stay full longer.

- **Eggs** - Healthy protein helps us feel full and regulates hunger and fullness signals. Limit to 7 whole eggs in a week to stay heart fit.

Yogurt - Protein-packed, full of probiotics that promote gut health and weight loss, high in calcium, and a source of healthy carbs.

- Choose yogurt with limited sugar content.

- **Salmon** - All forms of fish offer healthy protein, and certain fish like salmon provide healthy fats.

- **Whole grains** - While fad diets often give grains a bad rap, whole grains provide an important source of fiber, B vitamins (thiamin, riboflavin, niacin and folate) and many minerals (phosphorus, zinc, copper, iron, magnesium, and selenium). They're also known to reduce the risk of obesity, so include modest portions multiple times daily. Choices include whole-grain bread products, oats, quinoa, brown/black/red/wild rice, barley, and wheat berries.

- **Chia Seeds** - A great source of healthy fat and fiber, which helps ensure our stable energy and mood.

- Add to most any meal for a nutritious boost.

- **Soybeans** - Also known as edamame (ay-duh-MAH-may), science shows soybeans and foods made from them, including tofu and tempeh, are high in protein, fiber, antioxidants and plant sterol, a compound that naturally lowers cholesterol. Ready-to-eat choices include soymilk, shelled edamame, and seasoned tempeh.

- **Berries** - Any variety works. Loaded with Flavonoids and Vitamin C, and high in fiber. Blend them into smoothies, yogurt, or eat them as a snack.

- **Flaxseed** - Each tablespoon of ground flaxseed contains about 1.8 grams of plant Omega-3s as well as Lignans, which have antioxidant qualities. Flaxseed contains up to 800 times more Lignans than other plant foods.

- **Kale** - A very good source of Vitamin A, Vitamin C, Vitamin K, Vitamin B6, Potassium, as well as Copper and Manganese. Consume raw, cooked, or blend into smoothies.

- **Almonds** - Nutrients include Vitamin E, Copper and Magnesium. Grab a handful daily for a high fiber, healthy fat with some protein.

- **Broccoli** - High in fiber, Vitamin E, Manganese, and Carotenoids. Enjoy raw or cooked.

- **Avocado** - Technically a fruit, avocados contain over 20 vitamins and minerals essential for heart health. Go easy on these, however, because they're loaded with monounsaturated fat. A ¼ of an avocado is a reasonable portion; otherwise, it's too much fat.

- **Cherries** - A cup provides 16% of the recommended vitamin C for the day. Not in season? Frozen or canned (avoid canned in heavy syrup as sugar is pro-inflammatory) have all the nutritional value of fresh.

- **Sweet Potatoes** - An excellent source of vitamin A, vitamin C, Manganese, Copper, Pantothenic acid, and Vitamin B6.

- **Citrus** - Load up on Vitamin C and Lycopene with oranges and grapefruit, and squeeze the juice of lemons and limes **into your water** each day to establish a heart-healthy routine of drinking 'super water'.

ACTION PLAN

Make a copy of this list of superfoods and tape it to your refrigerator, so you'll have it in front of you every time you reach for something to eat. Add more superfoods to the list as you learn more and experiment with them.

SOBERTUDE HABIT #16 — TAKE A HIKE

When you think about it, hiking is walking on a slant. There's certainly nothing complicated about it; it just requires a little more effort to walk uphill. But that uphill effort is what makes it even more effective than just walking on a flat surface. If you feel like you're in decent shape, it might be a good idea to "step up" your exercise routine by incorporating a short hike or two into your week.

Hopefully, you have some trails or hills near your home that you can access easily. Even if you have to drive a short distance, finding a safe outdoor hiking trail is worth the extra effort.

Hiking is great for every part of your body, including your leg muscles (your calves in particular), back muscles, stomach, and side muscles, as well as your cardio condition. You will probably notice that it takes a shorter period of time to feel fatigued, especially your legs, when you first start hiking. And you'll probably feel out of breath faster as well. The uphill angle adds a higher degree of pressure and difficulty to your body than walking on a flat surface does. But that's the point. You want to start increasing your strength and endurance, and hiking is a great way to start.

Equally important, hiking allows you to explore the outdoors beyond your neighborhood. Getting out into nature is one of the best gifts you can give yourself. The air is generally cleaner, the views are more beautiful, and it provides the perfect setting to clear your mind and release stress, depression, and anxiety.

You don't need to overexert yourself, ether. Start slowly and take your time. Stop if you feel fatigued or out of breath. And never miss an opportunity to pause and look around at the nature that surrounds you. This is usually the best part of hiking, admiring the natural world.

Hiking is especially enjoyable with a companion. Ask a friend, spouse, child, or your dog to join you. By adding an easy hike into your routine once per week, you will be on your way to a much healthier body, mind, and spirit.

ACTION PLAN

In addition to bringing water on every hike, buy a good pair of hiking shoes or sneakers that are comfortable, and offer good support. Good shoes aren't inexpensive, but they're well worth the investment over time.

- **I plan to go hiking for _____ minutes 1/2/3 times (circle one) this week.**

- **I plan to go hiking for _____ minutes 1/2/3 times (circle one) next week.**

Example: *I plan to go hiking for 45 minutes 2 times this week*

SOBERTUDE HABIT #17 — GET 8 HOURS OF SLEEP

Sleep is critical to good health. The average adult requires 7-8 hours of sleep every night to feel rested. Unfortunately, many of us choose to ignore this simple fact, instead opting to stay up late watching TV, trolling the internet, or doing a host of other non-essential activities to fill our time.

A great deal of medical research has focused on how sleep affects the human body. Suffice it to say that sleep is crucial to longevity, physical wellness, and psychological well-being. The plain and simple fact is that if you don't get enough sleep each night, you're going to feel terrible. And if minimal sleep becomes habitual, the long-term impact can be devastating to your health and happiness.

How does a proper amount of sleep impact your life, according to medical research?

- Lowers your blood pressure

- Improves your mental acuity

- Improves your concentration

- Improves your mood

- Improves your immune system

- Improves athletic ability

- Relieves stress and anxiety
- Reduces depression
- Regulates your body weight
- Reduces your chance of having a heart attack or stroke
- Makes you a nicer person

For many people, getting a proper amount of sleep each night is difficult because they have active brains continually pestering them with negative thoughts. One way to combat the negative brainstorm that might be keeping you awake is by practicing meditation each night before bedtime (see Sobertude Habit #3). Meditation, when practiced regularly, can significantly reduce the chatter in your brain and calm your spirit. Exercise and yoga are good ways to calm the body and mind before sleep (see Sobertude Habit #11).

Consuming too much sugar (or caffeine) before bedtime will also impact your ability to sleep. Therefore, it's best to avoid any foods that contain sugar or caffeine at least 3 hours before going to bed.

You should establish a *regular sleep schedule* by going to bed *at the same time each night.* There are also various all-natural sleep aids, such as melatonin, you can find at most health food stores that can help you achieve a full night of sleep.

Sleep is essential to your health and state-of-mind. Find out why you might not be getting the proper amount of sleep each night, at least 7-8 hours, then develop a plan to resolve the problem. Your body (and your friends and family) will thank you for it every morning.

ACTION PLAN

To solve any problem, it helps to see the problem on paper. Start a sleep journal and track what time you go to bed and what time you wake up in the morning. Identify what might be keeping you awake (negative thoughts, anxiety, too much caffeine, etc.). Then create a resolution plan to overcome any obstacles that might be blocking you from sleep.

Sleep Journal Example:

- *Night #1 - Went to bed past midnight. Restless all night. Too many negative thoughts. I toss and turn all night until 6:00 am. Feel like crap all day.*

- *Night #2 - Went to bed past midnight. Ate chocolate cake at 10:30 pm. Too wired to sleep all night. I toss and turn until 5:30 am. No energy at work.*

- *Night #3 - Went to bed past midnight. Feeling depressed . I toss and turn until 7:30 am. Grumpy and short tempered around the family all day.*

Example Resolution Plan:

- *I will take a 15-minute walk and meditate for 15 minutes 1 hour before bedtime.*

- *I will commit to going to bed every night at 10:00 pm*

- *I will avoid all sugar and caffeine 3 hours before bedtime.*

SOBERTUDE HABIT #18 — TAKE A DAILY SUPPLEMENT

You should get the majority of your essential nutrients and vitamins directly from the food you eat. If we're eating a diet that consists of primarily fresh, organic fruits, vegetables, and lean protein, your body will thrive, and your health will improve. However, there are times when certain supplements can contribute to your health.

Visit your local health food store and explore the wide variety of exotic supplements filling the shelves. You can experiment with a host of vitamins and supplements. Be aware that vitamins and supplements can be expensive. So the best approach, when getting started, is to keep it to the simple list provided below. Most importantly, for safety reasons, never buy any vitamins or supplements made in China, India, or any country other than the United States, Canada, or Western Europe where manufacturing regulations are generally strict.

To get started, consider the following:

- **Multi-Vitamins** – A multivitamin should be the cornerstone of your supplement plan. Find one that offers a broad blend of essential nutrients and vitamins. A good brand is Nature Made, but there are many to choose from with a variety of prices that you can find in any grocery store or online.

- **Vitamin C** – Essential for the repair and growth of every tissue in your body.

- **Fish Oil** – Get your daily dose of Omega-3's. One of the best things you can take every day is a small dose of natural, organic fish oil. Helps with heart health, digestion, skin and hair repair, liver function, and supports weight loss.

- **Non-Flush Niacin** – Take for high cholesterol. Be careful of taking regular Niacin (versus non-flush), which may cause flushing and hot flashes. Stick with the non-flush variety.

These are just a few suggestions that offer positive health benefits. If you're able to find a good supplement or natural food store in your area, explore the aisles and learn everything you can. You can also pick up an enormous amount of information on the internet, but beware of snake oil sales pitches for junk vitamins from disreputable companies.

ACTION PLAN

To complement a healthy lifestyle that includes regular exercise and sleep, explore your local health store for the supplements suggested above and others.

- **Go online and research various vitamins and supplements.**

- **Write down any supplements that match your current health needs.**

- **Plan a trip to the local health store to explore your options.**

SOBERTUDE HABIT #19 — TAKE A CLASS

Too often, as we become adults and face the responsibilities of working, paying taxes, and raising families, we forsake our innate desire to learn. We become so entangled in day-to-day survival mode, focusing our attention on making ends meet, that we stop seeking more knowledge and skills.

One of the best things about childhood is the fact that we're always learning and growing. Perhaps this is one of the reasons many people hold fond memories of childhood because it's during this phase of our development that we're the most stimulated and excited. After all, the world is offering us so many new things to learn and enjoy.

Human beings are naturally curious creatures. We are at our happiest when we're acquiring new ideas and growing intellectually, spiritually, and artistically. People are not designed to stagnate in repetitive endeavors. People are designed to grow, develop, and learn continually. Otherwise, what's the point of being alive if we're not learning new things and taking advantage of the miraculous organ called a "brain?"

Now might be a good time to stimulate your brain by taking a class on any topic that interests you. Classes are offered in almost every town or city in the country, either privately, through local community colleges or adult learning centers, as well as online.

Best of all, as an adult, you usually don't have to worry about being accepted or passing a test to participate. You only have to show up and start learning. Often these classes are free or charge a minimal fee.

Is there anything you want to learn? Do you want to acquire a new skill or pursue a creative desire? You can probably find a class in your area covering almost any topic, including, but not limited to:

- Cooking
- Music
- Writing
- Business
- Photography
- Computers
- Dance
- Art appreciation
- Painting
- Sculpting
- Science
- Astronomy

Just because you're an adult doesn't mean you need to stop learning. The older you get, the more exciting it becomes to expand your wisdom and absorb more knowledge. Take the opportunity of re-experiencing the best part of childhood by merely taking a class and tapping into your natural curiosity as a human being.

ACTION PLAN

- Make a short list of topics or subjects that interest you.

- Search for classes in your community or online that cover your favorite topics.

- Enroll in 1 class this month. Don't overwhelm yourself by joining too many classes in the beginning. Just keep things simple by joining 1 or 2 classes to start.

SOBERTUDE HABIT #20 – ENJOY HERBAL TEAS

Enjoying daily herbal teas can have a very healthy and calming effect on your body. Even if you drink coffee in the morning, incorporating herbal tea into your life is a wise and enjoyable habit to develop each day.

Herbal teas are entirely natural and contain a variety of vitamins, minerals, and antioxidants that offer a multitude of health benefits. Herbal teas can improve digestion, boost immunity, lower blood pressure, and improve your skin's condition. Best of all, herbal teas can *reduce stress and anxiety*. There are even herbal teas to help you fall asleep at night.

Your local health food store or grocery store will have many herbal teas to explore and try. There seems to be an herbal tea for just about everything imaginable; liver health, digestion, constipation, muscle aches, anxiety, energy, nausea, allergies, heartburn, sleep. If there's a human ailment, there's probably an herbal tea for it.

Herbal teas come in a wide variety of interesting flavors and fragrances. There's a reason why herbal teas are so immensely popular around the world; they're delicious, soothing, and healthy. Add honey or stevia, and they become a sweet beverage any time of day.

Some of the most popular teas include:

- English Breakfast
- Earl Grey
- Darjeeling
- Green Tea
- White Tea
- Oolong
- Jasmin
- Chamomile
- Sleepy Time

Green tea, in particular, has powerful health benefits. The nutrients and compounds in green teas are crucial to your body and health. If you were to choose only one kind of tea to drink, green tea is the one to pick. Do yourself a favor and start drinking green tea or herbal tea every day.

ACTION PLAN

- **Take the time to explore herbal teas at your local store or online.**
- **Focus in particular on green teas as you get started.**
- **Drink herbal teas often, several times per day, if possible.**
- **Add natural sweeteners like honey, agave syrup, or stevia.**
- **Avoid caffeinated teas at night.**
- **Consider replacing your morning coffee with herbal teas that contain caffeine (Earl Grey, English Breakfast, etc.)**

SOBERTUDE HABIT #21 — PRAY DAILY

You don't have to be a religious person to benefit from prayer. You just have to keep an open mind and accept that perhaps you're not in control of the universe. Everyone needs a little help from time to time (some of us more than others).

Prayer is a way to release your anxieties and fears into the universe, like releasing a helium balloon into the sky. Once you release your anxiety-balloon into the air, you will often feel a tremendous sense of relief and calm.

There are numerous emotional benefits to prayer. Some are obvious, while some are more subtle. One thing you might have discovered is that you're not always in control of life. Life often just happens, taking you in whatever direction it wants despite your best efforts. Prayer is a way to remind yourself that you're not actually in charge of the universe. In fact, you might not be in charge of much other than your immediate actions right now. Accepting this fact can be liberating.

We often try to control everything about life, especially the outcomes. But when things don't turn out exactly as we plan, which is usually the case, we grow angry, frustrated, and resentful. We think to ourselves: *if I could just get my hands gripped tightly around life's throat, I could strangle it into submission and achieve everything I want and deserve.* But when we don't get everything we want in life, the resentment grows, and we become a walking pity-party.

Trying to control life is like trying to drink the ocean. It's impossible. We have to learn how *to live life on life's terms.* Life has its way of working out and often goes in a direction we don't anticipate. To quote John Lennon: "Life is what happens while you're busy making other plans."

This concept is important to embrace. Should you still make plans for the future? Yes, of course. Should you have ambition for things you want to achieve in life? Yes, absolutely. But the key is to recognize that your plans, however small or grandiose, are only ideas, not results. Try your best in everything you do, but leave the results to God to decide the outcome.

Prayer is an opportunity to turn your will, your life, and the outcome of your actions over to something other than yourself. The benefits of prayer are numerous and don't require much effort. Imagine if you could go to the gym for just a few minutes every day and get in fantastic physical shape. That's kind of how a few minutes of prayer each day can help you. But instead of ripped abs and bulging biceps, you'll achieve something better and longer-lasting: serenity and peace of mind.

Benefits of prayer Include:

- Communication with the source of life

- An opportunity to express humility and gratitude

- A way to search for answers and direction

- A chance to align your will with God's will

- A moment to release your ego and pride

- A source of emotional and physical strength

- A time to clarify your desires and goals (whatever the outcome might be)
- A way to find motivation and inspiration
- A way to accept life on life's terms
- A way to find peace

ACTION PLAN

Pray daily, as many times per day as you wish. Whether or not you pray on your knees is irrelevant. You can pray in bed while walking, hiking, or working. The idea is to open a pathway to spirit by expressing thanks for what you have, how you can serve others, and what you need. Keep it simple, and always be direct. You don't have to use flowery, biblical words, and phrases. Just speak the way you normally talk (either silently or out loud) and try to express gratitude, even when you don't feel grateful. You'll be amazed at how powerful and life-changing expressing gratitude in prayer can be.

SOBERTUDE HABIT #22 — PRAY FOR SUCCESS

Everyone has their interpretation of what the word "success" means. It can be applied to so many situations that it becomes difficult to define. Often we think of success as a measure of financial net worth or earning power. The size of someone's bank account or house is often the way we decide if someone is successful. But this is a very narrow view of the word and focuses only on one aspect of a person's life. Our lives are much more complex and layered to simply focus on how much money we have to decide whether we're "successful" or not.

Is a single mother who raises healthy, well-adjusted children entirely on her own less successful than a man who runs a Fortune 500 company? Is a teenage boy who joyfully participates in the Special Olympics less successful than a college student who gets drafted into the NFL? Is a heroin addict who gets clean then goes on to earn a degree in social work less successful than a person who gets elected to the US senate?

If you take a different view of the word *success*, you'll soon realize that it's a relative term that can be applied to many different situations in life.

Praying for success doesn't necessarily mean asking for financial rewards. Instead, it means asking for personal excellence in every part of your life. Success is often measured by how good a spouse

69

you are, how good a son or daughter you are, how good a sibling you are, or whether you're willing to help someone that day. Simply being kind is a form of success.

When you work, give it everything you have without worrying about the results. When you go to bed at night, know that you lived a full life that day and did as many things as you could to learn and grow. When you go to sleep, know that you tried your best every minute of the day, no matter how things turned out.

Don't measure success solely by the number of dollars in your bank account (for some of us, a minimal measurement). Instead, find success in your attitude, outlook, and behavior. Seek success not just in financial gain, but in mental and spiritual gain as well.

ACTION PLAN

During your daily prayer (see Sobertude Habit # 21), ask for the ability to recognize and appreciate success in all forms, not just financially. Pray for a willingness to be the best person you can be that day and to make yourself available to help others whenever possible.

Example Prayer:

God, today may I be successful in everything I do.

May I be the best that I can be.

May I always be kind to others and to myself

May I be kind and compassionate to every living being.

May I work hard and not worry about the results.

May I live life on life's terms and be filled with joy,

Knowing that I tried my best every step of the way.

SOBERTUDE HABIT #23 — SEEK SPIRITUAL WEALTH

The word wealth, like success, is a relative term that can be applied to many different things. Financial wealth is the most prominent and common way to use the word. But often, our spiritual bank account feels empty. We become emotionally impoverished to the point that we can become depressed and frustrated by life with all of its challenges. For some people, this inner-bankruptcy leads to addiction, self-abuse, isolation, and in extreme cases, even suicide. But we have access to an abundance of spiritual riches that can be found in prayer and meditation.

Material wealth is nothing to be ashamed of, nor is there is anything wrong or sinful about money or financial wealth. Money is just a means by which you can obtain and exchange goods and labor and enjoy some of the luxuries that the world offers. It's neither good nor bad. But to seek happiness from money alone is usually futile because no matter how much money you have if you're sad or depressed on the inside, a new house or car or shiny piece of jewelry won't ease your suffering for more than an hour or maybe a day. It's a temporary fix when what you really need is long-lasting, deeply felt spiritual fulfillment.

What is spiritual wealth?

- Spiritual wealth is feeling unified with God or Spirit.

- Spiritual wealth is feeling connected to all life on earth.

- Spiritual wealth is recognizing your value as a human being.

- Spiritual wealth is feeling serene even in times of turmoil.

- Spiritual wealth is feeling calm, even in times of chaos.

- Spiritual wealth is your capacity to feel joy at being alive.

- Spiritual wealth is feeling gratitude for your blessings.

- Spiritual wealth is feeling love for yourself and others.

The list could go on much further, and you can certainly add your ideas to what spiritual wealth means to you. But the point to remember is that while material wealth can solve certain types of problems, spiritual wealth gives life meaning and purpose.

Take the time to look for the deeper parts of life that bring joy to you and others. Seek out experiences that are neither material nor earth-bound. Instead, learn how to recognize and appreciate the moments that come from spiritual experiences, moments of transcendence that are rich with serenity, love, and positivity emotion.

ACTION PLAN

Identifying the riches of spiritual experience can be as easy as simply enjoying the sound of someone laughing, a child perhaps, or the beauty found in nature. Take the time to look for things around you and inside you that feel uplifting and transcendent. Savor the feeling as long as it lasts and carry it forward through the rest of your day, even sharing it with others.

SOBERTUDE HABIT #24 —
READ SPIRITUAL BOOKS

Reading is one of the most fulfilling habits you can develop. The world is full of books on every known topic imaginable. If you don't often read (*thank you for reading this book*), do yourself a favor and develop a simple plan to read a few pages from any kind of book each day. Whether you prefer fiction or nonfiction books, reading is one of the absolute best ways to fill your time and your head with new knowledge.

Spiritual books should be of a primary source of information and learning if you're interested in developing a deeper awareness and wonder about the world and the human condition. Whether you read books on Buddhism, Christianity, or any other spiritually-themed subject, spiritual books will guide you toward a better understanding of life, emotions, faith, and even the nature of love better than any other art form.

The spiritual book industry, including the self-help category, has been thriving and growing for a long time. There's a reason for this; people are looking to learn and share information about life and existence more intimately and profoundly than what is offered in movies, television, or schools. Human beings are naturally curious and want to explore the hidden parts of life, including the nature of the soul and the creation of life.

We all know, deep down inside, that there is much more to life than going to work and paying taxes. There is a hidden universe of emotions, ideas, and energy buried within each of us, no matter how cynical or jaded we become. Spiritual books offer a simple and often intense way to reach into the lower depths of our soul so we can explore what others have experienced in their search for meaning.

One way to enjoy the power of spiritual books is to read a few pages or chapters every night before going to sleep. This is particularly potent because many of the ideas you absorb in your reading will have a chance to germinate and grow in your mind while you're dreaming. There is also a great deal of comfort that can be experienced when reading certain types of spiritual books before sleep, especially books on faith, God, and love.

Instead of falling to sleep watching reruns of old war movies or, worst of all, watching the news (please do yourself a favor and don't watch the news before going to sleep), enjoy the intimate and comforting knowledge you will absorb from spiritual books.

ACTION PLAN

Reading spiritual books doesn't take a considerable time commitment. Just spend 10-15 minutes per day reading spiritual-themed books every day. If you prefer, just read five pages per day. You will be surprised how many books you'll be able to read every year by just devoting a few minutes daily (or nightly) to reading.

- **I'm interested in the following three spiritual topics (Example: *The nature of God; The power of positivity; Buddhist meditation*.):**

- **I will read for _____ (minutes) every night before bed.**

SOBERTUDE HABIT #25 — PRACTICE ACCEPTANCE

Learning to live in acceptance is the key to living a life of peace and serenity. The term "acceptance" doesn't mean "resignation," which implies giving up or allowing bad things to happen. Acceptance, as we want to use the word, means *non-resistance*. You want to be able to reach a point when you can *accept* things that happen in your life and observe them without fear or judgment.

If I can borrow a well-worn sports analogy, life throws you a lot of curveballs. If you become too fixated or attached to how things SHOULD BE instead of accepting how of things ACTUALLY ARE, you become trapped in a never-ending cycle of disappointment and frustration. It often seems that your problems appear out of nowhere. You might start the day with a particular set of expectations, only to be thrown a curveball that catches you off guard, sometimes hitting you square in the face.

Some days you're hit by multiple curve balls traveling at tremendous speed. Then you find yourself trying to fix one problem while confronting another and another. You become overwhelmed and can easily succumb to frustration and anger. You might want to throw your hands up in the air and resign yourself to your fate.

But there's another path you can take: **ACCEPTANCE.**

A great phrase to always remember whenever life throws you curve balls is, *"This too shall pass."*

The fact is, all things shall pass eventually. Nothing is permanent. Bad, unpleasant, or frightening things all end at some point. The same is true for good things. *All things shall pass.*

The trick is not to obsess over or become overly attached to anything, good or bad, but merely accept them as passing conditions.

One moment might seem perfect; the next moment might be filled with problems. One day you might be dating your soul mate; the next day your heart is broken. One week you might feel healthy; the next week you're sick. One month you might have money in the bank; the next month you're broke.

All of these are passing conditions. Nothing is permanent, and nothing stays the same. The only thing you can rely on is change itself. Change is the only constant. The bad things and the good things all pass into something else at some point. So lighten up and accept the ebb and flow of life.

If you can live in acceptance of **what is** and not **what should be**, you will find it much easier to live in harmony with the fluctuations and changes that confront us every day. You don't want to be doormats and let life (or people) trample over you. You have to take responsibility and fix things that need to be fixed. But it's also important to realize that life is filled with ups and downs and constant change. *Life just is.* When curveballs are bombarding you, simply remind yourself: *"This too shall pass."*

ACTION PLAN

Commit to memory the expression *"this too shall pass."* Write it down. Whenever life starts to beat you up or throw you curve-balls, recall the phrase, and repeat it as often as needed. If you repeat it and believe it, there are very few situations you won't be able to handle, no matter how difficult or daunting they might appear.

SOBERTUDE HABIT #26 – DEVELOP HUMILITY

First and foremost, humility is NOT the same as humiliation. People often confuse the two words. You don't want to practice humiliation - life is difficult enough already without feeling embarrassment or shame. On the other hand, humility is a willingness to feel profoundly grateful and accept that we're powerless against the storms of life while remaining content and serene. The sooner we admit that we're powerless, the faster we'll find comfort and peace. Humility is another opportunity to accept *life on life's terms instead of our own.*

Sometimes the best thing we can do for ourselves is to **LET GO**. It's amazing how liberating it can feel to say, *"I'm not in charge of the universe, so now I'm just going to let go of all my worries and fears and let life take me in whatever direction it chooses."*

The fact is, we're not in charge of much of anything. Realizing this fact is a gift. God is in charge. The universe is incomprehensibly vast. The world continues to turn every day. The forces of nature never cease. The sun rises, and the sunsets. And the reality is we don't have any control over any of it. Life is so vast and ever-changing that humankind has virtually no input. We're here for the ride, so enjoy the passing scenery.

Some people might think this sounds nihilistic or depressing. But it's the most joyous discovery you might find. To *let go and humble yourself* before God and the universe will lift a tremendous weight off your shoulders. To admit that you're not in charge of life and how it turns out, allows you to stop trying to force life to be what you think it should be. Instead, accept that life is spontaneous, different every day, and always surprising.

What's important is being prepared for every event that comes your way, good or bad, and accepting the outcome with grace, humor, and dignity.

Helping others is an excellent way to achieve a healthy sense of humility. Acknowledging the grace we've been granted in our lives is another. Instead of wailing and punching against the injustices of life, we can take a moment each day to humble ourselves before God or spirit, rejoicing in our humility and allowing ourselves to live *life on life's terms,* not our own. It might be the most liberating experience you ever discover.

ACTION PLAN

Sometimes the easiest and quickest way to achieve a spiritual goal is to say a simple prayer. Each morning, before you start your day, simply say a short prayer asking for the willingness to remain humble and gracious under every circumstance that greets you that day, good or bad. You can make up your prayer or use "The Serenity Prayer" to set the tone for the day:

The Serenity Prayer

God, grant me the serenity

To accept the things I cannot change,

Courage to change the things I can,

And the wisdom to know the difference

SOBERTUDE HABIT #27 — VISIT A HOUSE OF WORSHIP

Houses of worship are designed to conjure a sense of tranquility and transcendence. Whether you visit a church, synagogue, temple, or mosque, a house of worship is a sacred place that will elicit respect and awe in most people. Equally important, you don't need to be a religious person to enjoy the spiritual benefits you'll receive. Even hardened cynics and atheists will often experience a sense of humility and respect when they pass through the doors.

There are times when we just need a moment of respite from the chaos of the day. Visiting a church or temple is often an excellent way to simply breathe, spiritually, and enjoy a moment of solitude.

There are no requirements (usually) to entering a house of worship. Christian churches and Buddhist temples are particularly open to public visitation—both welcome everyone with open arms. Often the beauty and artistry of these places are enough to fill you with wonder and awe. If the opportunity is available, sit for a few minutes (or longer) in quiet prayer and meditation.

Often such places of worship are designed to block out all noise from the outside world, making it possible to listen to your breath and experience the rhythm of your heart beating in your chest. This is a wonderful opportunity to focus on gratitude and to count your blessings.

Whether or not you have any religious affiliation, take a few moments during the day or week, or even just once per month, to visit a local house of worship. Contemplate the soothing stillness and silence. Gaze at the beauty that surrounds you and enjoy the gentle beating of your own heart.

ACTION PLAN

Every town and city has a church or temple of some kind that you can visit. Set aside a few minutes to enter one near your home. Turn off your phone before entering, and don't bring anything that will distract you from quiet contemplation.

SOBERTUDE HABIT #28 — START A RAINY DAY FUND

As stated earlier, life often throws us curveballs, and we have to prepare and adjust for the sudden changes that eventually come our way. We should always plan for the future, set goals, and hope for the best outcome in every part of our lives. But sometimes bad things happen, and there's nothing we can do about it. Pray for the best, prepare for the worst.

This is especially true in your financial life. You should always be planning and saving for the future. But sometimes life is going to throw you curve balls like unexpected medical bills, car repairs, and sudden unemployment. When these issues come your way, you need to make sure to have some money set aside to meet the emergency.

You need to begin preparing for the inevitable rainy day that might soak you sometime in the future. It's a simple fact that hard times confront us all, so why not do your best to be ready for the downpour.

Decide on a small amount of money you can set aside for an emergency fund. It doesn't have to be a lot. Even just a dollar a day, or thirty dollars per month, is a good start. Ideally, you want to build an emergency fund worth approximately six months of living expenses. If this goal is not realistic for you, you can set a smaller, attainable goal of perhaps one hundred dollars, or five hundred dollars saved over the next six months. Even a small emergency fund of $500 can have a significant impact on your financial stability and emotional well-being when an emergency arises.

Open a savings account at a local bank. Set a goal to add a small amount to the account every week or month. Again, it can be just a few dollars. But get in the habit of setting aside something every week or month.

There will come a time when the rain starts to fall; it's a certainty. The sooner you prepare for the inevitable downpour, the better off you'll feel and the more likely you'll be able to get through any situation without significant disruption to your life. Start saving now, add to your rainy-day fund as often as possible, and over time you will have enough stashed away to meet almost any financial emergency.

ACTION PLAN

Create a simple plan to save a few dollars regularly. Start by opening a separate bank account (or credit union account) and commit to adding any amount you can afford weekly or monthly. Stay consistent and focus on saving six months of living expenses.

- **I will open a new account at (name of bank):**

- **I plan to contribute $_____ every week/month to the account**

- **My savings goal is $_____ over 6 months**

- **My savings goal is $_____ over 12 months**

- **My savings goals is $_____ over 24 months**

SOBERTUDE HABIT #29 — CREATE A BUDGET

Financial stress plays a significant factor in your spiritual and psychological serenity, so it's essential to set up a simple budget that is easy to follow and reduces your worries.

If you've ever owned or managed a business, you know that you have to continually track how much money you're making compared to how much you're spending. Whatever remains after costs is your profit (this is a very simplified description of a business profit-and-loss principle). It looks something like this:

$$\text{Income} - \text{Costs} = \text{Profit}$$

Again, this is a very simplified explanation of how a business tracks its finances. But it illustrates the concept in its most basic form, especially when applying it to your own life. It's essential to approach your personal finances in the same way. Get in the habit of running your financial life like a small business.

- **How much money do you have or make (income)?**

- **How much do you need to pay bills (costs)?**

- **How much will you have left after paying the bills (profit)?**

One of the easiest ways to get a bird's eye view of your finances is to get it all down on paper or an Excel spreadsheet. This will clarify where you came from (financially speaking), where you are now, and where you're going.

It's essential to create and track a simple budget. Track how much you need in your pocket, how much you need to meet your weekly obligations, and how much you need for monthly expenses. The idea is to track your budget so you have a clearer understanding of where you stand and where you will be daily, weekly, and monthly.

ACTION PLAN

The sooner you create a budget and track your finances, the happier you'll feel, especially when a financial curveball hits you. Set up a simple plan to track your income and expenses and review it at least 1x per week (or more often if you wish).

Create a 3 column overview of your finances:

Column 1) - How Much Money Do I Have Right Now (This should include what's in your pocket, what's in your drawers, what's in your bank account, or any type of savings or investment account, how much you earn weekly/monthly).

Column 2) - How Much Money Do I Owe (This should include all debt such as credit cards, car loans, mortgages, loans from friends and family, or any other debt)

Column 3) - How Much Money Do I Need for Bills (This should include any rent, car loans, utility bills, groceries, or any other recurring costs you need to pay each month to live).

SOBERTUDE HABIT #30 — INVEST IN YOUR FUTURE

Investing is a fascinating and complex topic that some people spend their entire professional lives studying. When some of us hear the word "investment," we think of stocks, bonds, and Wall Street. It often feels like an intimidating and esoteric subject that is better left to the experts.

However, investing is pretty simple as long as you stick to a few basic concepts and principles. In its most basic form, investing is merely taking a dollar that you earned, putting it somewhere safe, and allowing it to grow. There's a term you've probably heard called "Return on Investment" or "ROI," which succinctly summarizes your goal when investing; you invest your money in a business, bank, or stock, with a reasonable expectation of growth to be returned to you over time.

Investing in your future doesn't necessarily mean you must put your money into the stock market or a business hoping that it grows. You only need to set aside a small percentage of your income (10% - 15%). Then redirect it towards a **savings account** or a **money market fund**. Note: your "rainy day fund" that we discussed earlier should be considered a separate savings account dedicated strictly to future emergencies).

When you put money into a savings account or money market fund, you won't receive a high ROI. The average rate of return is around 1% - 2%, which is not exactly going to set your financial world on fire. But you have to start somewhere, and a 1% return on your investment is better than 0%.

If you only make $1,000 per month, try to put $10 - $15 in a savings account or money market fund. At first, it might seem like a ridiculously small amount to set aside, but it will add up over time. Remember, patience is your best friend when it comes to saving and investing.

Investing in your future serve two goals:

- Building wealth

- Reducing your financial stress and worry

ACTION PLAN

Your "rainy day fund" should be your first goal when it comes to saving. If you can afford to contribute to an emergency fund AND an investment fund, that's wonderful. But if you can only save into one right now, focus on your rainy day fund until you have saved six months of living expenses. Once you achieve that first goal, start a simple investment savings plan as follows:

- **Open a savings account or money market account.**

- **Invest 10-15% of your monthly income to this account.**

- **Be diligent, and try never to miss a month of contributions. .Whenever possible, contribute more than 15%.**

- **Watch your money grow and try not to spend it on anything for a few years.**

SOBERTUDE HABIT #31 — BE POLITE

The more conflict and drama you can remove from your life, the more joy and peace you will experience. One of the easiest ways to reduce friction and tension is by practicing good manners and polite social behavior. Being polite in every social situation, even when you don't feel like being polite, almost always has a positive impact on how you, and the people around you, feel.

Naturally, there will be times when you're in a particularly foul mood when the last thing you want to do is be courteous. We all have those days. However, it's essential to try your best to be polite even during your worst moments, because it makes other people feel good about themselves and you. Similar to dropping a pebble into a pond, the ripple effect of politeness and good manners goes a long way to spread positive vibes.

For some people, good manners are easy and natural. For others, it takes more conscious effort. Many of us have to train ourselves to be aware of how we're behaving in public, how we speak, and how courteous we're acting. We have to remind ourselves daily (sometimes hourly) to behave in a respectful, upbeat, and well-mannered way whenever we deal with other people.

You probably know someone who exhibits atrocious manners whenever they're around other people. They never make eye contact. They're inarticulate, rude, and grumpy no matter whom they offend. They don't put any effort into their appearance. They grumble, complain, and curse without considering those around them. They're socially inept and make you and other people feel uncomfortable and awkward whenever they enter a room. We all know people like this. We have to make sure WE'RE NOT THAT PERSON!

When you enter a room or situation, make the extra effort to put other people at ease. Make eye contact, greet people warmly, be extra friendly to everyone. This is particularly important during moments of stress or conflict. Politeness can act like a cool and calming breeze when the temperature of the room is rising to a boiling point. Equally important, the more polite you are to others, the more often they will treat you with respect in return. When everyone is polite, usually everyone wins.

ACTION PLAN

Make it a priority to remain conscious of how you're behaving in EVERY social setting. Always do your best to put other people at ease by acting with proper manners. Be friendly and courteous to everyone, and other people will reciprocate the gesture more often than not. And when someone isn't polite toward you, simply ignore them...*politely.*

SOBERTUDE HABIT #32 — PLANT SEEDS OF LOVE

There is no greater force in the universe than love. Without love, the mother would not feed her child. Without love, humankind would never have evolved beyond the grunting stage of cave dwellers. Without love, there would be no kindness or compassion in the world. Without love, we would have no reason to exist. Love is the nourishment that feeds our soul and illuminates our being. Love is the greatest force in the universe. Love gives life meaning.

And love is not exclusive to humans. All creatures on earth seem to have some capacity to give and receive love. Just ask anyone who owns a dog or cat. Or witness how primates care for one another. Love is the universal essence permeating all life on earth.

As the saying goes, *we reap what we sow*. And so it is with love. When we plant seeds of love, we reap the rewards of what we have sown. Love begets love just as anger begets anger and hate begets hate. To receive love, we first need to learn how to give love. It's not complicated, nor is it a revolutionary new idea. Humankind learned long ago that the power of love keeps us alive, fulfilled, and happy.

Start with the people closest to you, or people you encounter during the day. This doesn't mean you should throw your arms around strangers and hug them—no need to scare people. But you can wish only good things for others, even strangers. You can hope that their lives are joyous and serene. You can pray that they have lives filled with love and friendship. It's important to remember that everyone needs, wants, and deserves love. Even your enemies (or perceived enemies) can love and be loved. No creature on earth doesn't benefit from or want love.

So when you pray or interact with others, try to plant seeds of love in your mind for everyone. It may not change the world, but it will adjust your mind. You'll start to see people differently. You'll feel more empathy and compassion for others. In return, others will begin to feel the energy you're putting out and *return to you the seeds you have sown.*

ACTION PLAN

Planting seeds of love should be a daily habit you develop just like brushing your teeth or bathing (you brush your teeth and bathe daily, right?). Get in the habit of starting each day with a simple prayer or mental commitment to be loving and kind towards everyone you meet, no matter what. Even on days when you have to deal with rude or disrespectful people, try to find a kind word or thought about them. Replace all your anger and frustration with words and thoughts of love, even when you don't want to or don't feel like doing it.

Commit this simple prayer to memory. Say it in the morning before you leave the house and repeat it as often as necessary throughout each day:

A Prayer for Love

May I be loving, kind, and charitable to everyone I encounter.

May each person I meet find love and peace today and forever.

SOBERTUDE HABIT #33 —
BE OF SERVICE

Being of service to others is an excellent opportunity to get out of our heads and focus our attention away from ourselves. Too often, we become trapped in a never-ending cycle of inner-reflection and self-analysis, which can devolve into self-obsession and selfishness. Another way to put it is "analysis paralysis," when we spend so much time analyzing ourselves that we become spiritually or emotionally paralyzed. We should always do our best to look outward, beyond our own minds, to the world around us. The easiest way to do this is to seek opportunities to make ourselves available to serve others.

Not that inner-reflection is always a bad thing. It can be an important part of healing and recovery from many things, including addiction or emotional trauma. But we need to be careful not to get trapped in our inner world or face the danger of becoming isolated from the outer world. It's very easy to allow ourselves to wallow in self-reflection, whether we're thinking about how sad we are (*"woe-is-me-ism"*) or how great we are (*"damn-I'm-awesome-ism"*).

If you can simply start each day with the question, *"How can I be of service to others today?"* you'll be amazed at how many opportunities will appear in your daily life to help others. Putting the question into the universe is enough to spark an *acute awareness* of those around you who might be in distress.

You don't have to save the world or cure cancer. Typically, it's just a matter of showing a small kindness, perhaps talking to someone who feels sad or lonely, or offering a genuine compliment, or giving a ride to someone who doesn't own a car. There are countless ways you can be of service to others every day, and by making it a daily priority, the opportunities will be present.

ACTION PLAN

Always be on the lookout for how you can help someone. Start each day with the question, *"How can I be of service to others today?"* Do you know an elderly neighbor who needs a ride to the store? Do you have a friend who might need some advice or comfort after experiencing a recent heartbreak? Make it a point to try to help at least one person every day. Even just a small compliment or a ride to the store is an opportunity to be of service to someone in need.

SOBERTUDE HABIT #34 — DON'T COMPARE YOURSELF TO OTHERS

We all do it from time to time. We see someone we admire, or perhaps know someone who *seems* cooler than us or has all the good stuff like fancy cars or a big house. There's that little spark of envy that twinkles in our brain, telling us we would be happier if we were just like that person. *If only my life were more like (fill in name here), then I'd be happy! My life would be perfect and complete!*

Envy is a common trait in humans. Most people experience envy at some point or another in their life. We often take it too far, continually comparing ourselves to other people and what they have and how amazing their lives seem to be as if they're living in a non-stop orgy of perfection and delight.

Social media doesn't help, either. Platforms like Facebook, Instagram, and YouTube encourage us to share our lives in front of the world. But we rarely share all the boring stuff we do like washing dishes or cleaning laundry. Instead, everyone posts the most exciting (and often staged) parts of their lives. It's easy to feel envy and jealousy when it seems like everyone else is on a constant tropical vacation swimming with dolphins while we're at home scrubbing dirty plates and folding socks.

Don't compare yourself to others. Recognize that everyone, no matter how exciting their life might *seem*, deals with as much "normal" stuff as you. Nobody's life is devoid of tedium or frustration, no matter how many exciting pictures they post on Facebook. Everyone has to deal with the day-to-day doldrums of work, chores, and responsibilities. Even the Queen of England has to roll out of bed in the morning with stiff muscles, put on socks (*do Queen's wear socks?*), brush her teeth, and deal with headaches, hangnails and indigestion just like everyone else. No one's life is perfect, not even a monarch's.

Always remember that each person is unique in their own way, including you. Everyone has something positive to contribute to the world. Envying what other people seem to have (which is often an illusion) is guaranteed to create jealousy in you, which can be a very destructive emotion.

Instead, when you see someone who seems to have a better life or owns more stuff, simply be happy for them. Don't envy them, applaud them. Their experience in life isn't your experience. Your life belongs to you and you alone, in all of its imperfection and beauty. Celebrate what you have, not what you don't have. Look for the unique parts of your life, no matter how small, and hold them close to your heart. Be proud of what makes you unique and special without comparing yourself to what others might have.

ACTION PLAN

Take the time to list out things in your life that are unique and make you happy. Look for special skills or talents you have or people in your life that bring you joy. Whenever you feel envy or jealousy rising in you for what someone else seems to have, remind yourself of the special parts of your life that make you unique. Most importantly, replace envy with gratitude whenever it appears.

- **Make a list of 5 (or more) things that are special to you and make you happy** (Example: *my kids, my faith, my garden, our home, my spouse*):

SOBERTUDE

- Every day review your list of what you HAVE, not what you don't have.

- Continually add to your list whenever you recognize a new one.

- Whenever envy or jealousy arises, review your list of what makes your life unique and special, and replace envy with gratitude.

SOBERTUDE HABIT #35 — DON'T BE A DOORMAT

Being a "people pleaser" can have a destructive impact on our mental and emotional well-being, just like envy and jealousy. Continually trying to make everyone else happy, at the cost of your happiness, is something to avoid in your daily life. If you spend too much time ALWAYS trying to make everyone like you, you risk becoming a human doormat, allowing others to step over you at the expense of your dignity and self-worth.

Wanting others to like us is natural. We all want to be liked, loved, admired, and desired. Humans are tribal beings, social animals who seek the comfort and companionship of others. But we often become obsessed with wanting others to like and love us to the point where we become fawning and obsequious. To put it less poetically, we become ass-kissers. No one likes an ass-kisser, and ass-kissers usually get mistreated and abused by the rest of the tribe. This is most obvious amongst children, especially during the High School years. Kids who try too hard at pleasing their peers often end up being shunned and lonely because of their evident desperation.

But it's not just kids who display clinging behavior. Many adults try too hard at pleasing everyone around them, desperate to be liked and loved, to the point that they become human doormats, stepped upon by everyone who passes their way.

It's vital to retain your dignity and independence under every circumstance. Never allow yourself to become so desperate for others to notice or love you that they end up walking over you and treating you poorly.

There are several places where ass-kissing and people-pleasing occur most often:

- Romantic relationships

- New friendships

- Jobs

- School

There are other areas of life when people-pleasing can become a problem, but these are the most common scenarios. Whenever you're in any of these situations, ask yourself if you're trying too hard to get people to recognize, like, or love you? Are you giving too much of yourself but receiving too little in return? Do you feel humiliated by your actions or desperate to make others acknowledge you?

When these moments arise, which they do for all of us at times, check yourself and stop whatever you're doing. Sometimes the best action, when we feel disrespected or humiliated, is to simply walk away from a situation or person if we realize we're giving more than we're receiving. If you're desperate to make someone want you or like you, that's when you might have to stop in your tracks, turn and walk away. Your dignity and self-worth are far too valuable to allow yourself to be someone else's doormat.

ACTION PLAN

Be on the lookout for the feeling of *desperation* whenever you're interacting with other people. When you detect a feeling in your gut that you might be trying just a little too hard to please someone or make them like you, whether it's an employer, a lover, or a friend, it's time to slow down and back off. Give them some space and attend to your feelings instead of worrying about their feelings. Keep your dignity intact always, and disengage from anyone who treats you with anything less than respect and courtesy.

SOBERTUDE HABIT #36 – CHECK YOUR POSTURE

How we stand, sit, or walk reflects how we feel. When we're sad, we often hang our heads and drop our shoulders. When we're bored, we slouch in our chair. When we feel unconfident or depressed, we walk hunched over, hands in our pockets, eyes staring at the ground.

However, when we feel happy, we hold our heads up and our shoulders back. When we're excited, we sit up straight in our chair, attentive and alert. When we feel confident and proud, we walk with an extra pep in our step, arms swinging joyfully at our sides, eyes gazing at the horizon with anticipation.

How you carry yourself, how you walk into a room, or present yourself to the world is expressed through body language. The equation looks like this:

- **Feeling bad = Bad posture**

- **Feeling good = Good posture**

Just as emotions are expressed through body language, you can also improve how you feel by improving your posture. The equation then looks like this:

- **Feeling bad = Good posture**

- **Feeling good = Good posture**

SOBERTUDE HABIT #36 – **CHECK YOUR POSTURE**

There is a great deal of back and forth communication between your body and your brain. On some days, your brain is in charge, while other days, your body is the captain of the ship. Your body has a powerful influence on your brain activity.

- When you take a warm shower, your brain feels comfort and ease.

- When you get a massage or meditate, your brain calms down.

- When you exercise, your brain feels excitement.

- When you eat chocolate or have sex, your brain floods with pleasure.

- When you sleep, your brain rests.

How you carry yourself, how you sit, stand, and walk, will have an immediate impact on your emotions and state of mind. If you train yourself to check your posture at all times, you'll feel and express confidence and self-respect under most circumstances. In turn, your emotional and psychological state will respond accordingly; on days when you're not feeling good, you can reverse how you're feeling by merely improving your posture. In effect, your brain will listen to your body.

You can test this theory easily by simply committing an entire day to slouching, hanging your head, staring at the ground, and walking with hunched shoulders. You're guaranteed to feel tired and depressed by the end of the day. To prove the theory in reverse, spend a day **standing upright**, sit with your **head held high**, keep your **eyes raised** at the horizon, and **walk with purpose and confidence**. You're guaranteed to feel more energetic and optimistic at the end of the day.

ACTION PLAN

Check your posture all the time. **Be aware of how you stand, sit, and walk.** Improve the communication between your body and brain by adjusting your posture throughout the day. When you catch yourself slouching in your chair, sit upright. When you catch yourself walking with drooping shoulders, straighten up and walk with confidence. When you catch yourself standing with arms crossed and eyes down, open your arms and gaze out at the world with dignity. Once you train yourself to become aware of your posture, you'll quickly influence how your brain and emotions respond.

SOBERTUDE HABIT #37 — USE POSTIVE LANGUAGE

We all know the children's rhyme that states: *"Sticks and stones may break my bones, but words will never hurt me."*

Really? Does anyone actually believe that? How many friendships, relationships, and marriages have been destroyed by cruel words that can't be taken back? How many jobs have been lost by employees shouting derogatory words at employers? How many people have been injured or killed as a result of racial hate-speech? How many wars have been started between countries because politicians stir up fear in the citizenry? Politicians use divisive language every day to demonize their opponents. Politics has become a verbal blood sport.

Language and the words we speak (and write) matter. Words have energy, and when misused, often lead to pain, suffering, and destruction. Likewise, the same power in words can enlighten and inspire people and improve the world. If words were harmless, as the children's rhyme implies, we would not need literature or music lyrics. Words fill our lives with positive energy as well as negative energy. Words are what separate us from the other creatures of the earth. Words can be either beautiful or ugly, depending on how they're used.

To use an extreme example, one of the most tragic misuses of language resulted, ultimately, in World War II and the Holocaust.

Adolph Hitler was a mastermind at using language to rally political power. Over several years, his use of language led the German people into a frenzy of hatred and prejudice, resulting in war and tens of millions of lives.

Once you become consciously aware of the power behind words, the more likely (I hope) that you will choose the language that offers joy, hope, and positivity to people around you. Instead of offering words of bitterness and anger, choose words carefully and words that enlighten and inspire others.

Using positive language is a crucial habit to develop for three main reasons:

- **Like your body language, verbal language influences how you feel. Your emotions and feelings are much improved, or impaired, by the words you speak.**

- **Words have a direct and immediate impact on the people around you. Harsh, cruel, or disrespectful language will result in negative energy between you and others.**

- **Bad or ugly language makes other people feel uncomfortable.**

We all use bad language from time to time. Bad language can be funny and often serves a purpose when we need to make a serious statement or point. But usually, negative language and words will result in negative energy and bad feelings. Instead, become aware of the words you use when you're speaking so that you can try to add a little more positive energy to the world. You'll feel better, and the people around you will feel better, too.

ACTION PLAN

Like your posture, be aware of the words that leave your mouth. Make it a point to check yourself before you speak. And when you talk, make a mental note whenever you use foul or negative language. Moving forward, try to use words that encourage others and offer beauty instead of ugliness and positivity instead of negativity. And when you can't find anything positive or helpful to say, it's a good time not to say anything.

SOBERTUDE HABIT #38 — LIVE FOR TODAY

One of the most common character defects many people share is a desire for immediate gratification. We want everything RIGHT NOW! Many of us tend to be very impatient. We're always in a hurry to get somewhere, even when we don't know where we want to go. The only thing we do know is we want it fast, and we want it NOW! We want the fix, and we want it NOW! *Give it to me no, now, now!*

Life is a journey, not a destination. All we have is today. Many of us have to train ourselves to be calm and patient and enjoy each moment, even when our brain is screaming for instant fulfillment and pleasure.

It's important to appreciate each moment and each day, recognizing that the moment you're in right now, this very second, is your life. Neither the past nor the future exist, they are simply ideas you either remember or anticipate. If you can learn to stay conscious of each moment, you will develop a better appreciation of life in the present rather than the past or future. This can have a very positive impact on your state of mind and emotional well-being. Instead of always worrying and stressing-out about what "could have been" or what "might happen," you can learn to enjoy the present moment instead.

One of the best books you can read on this topic is called the "Power of Now" by Eckhart Tolle. It teaches, in a clear and straightforward way, that our lives exist in the moment, and we must learn to appreciate and enjoy each current experience and not worry about the past or future stress.

This concept holds true in every part of your life. It's essential to take your time and remember that nothing good happens in a hurry. As they say, Rome wasn't built in a day. Learn to slow things down. Take it easy. Stay in the moment. Appreciate today. The only thing that you can do is try to improve a little one day at a time. Over time, the cumulative effects of your efforts make the difference as you move forward in life.

ACTION PLAN

Try to stay consciously aware of what you're doing in each moment of each day. Even tedious chores can start to seem enjoyable if you take the time to focus on what you're doing. Pick up a copy of Eckhart Tolle's book **The Power of Now**.

Memorize this quote from Bill Keane: *"Yesterday's the past, tomorrow's the future, but today is a gift. That's why it's called the present."*

SOBERTUDE HABIT #39 — NOURISH YOUR SOUL

We must empty our minds of negative thoughts each day, replacing dark thoughts and ideas with positive, uplifting reminders of how interesting, amusing, and wondrous life can be. The point is to feed your souls with nourishing words that provide uplifting and transcendent thoughts and ideas.

To repeat a metaphor we used earlier, if you were to take a glass filled with dirty, brown pond water and hold it under a dripping faucet, the drops of water from the sink would eventually replace the dirty pond water. The glass would then be filled with water clean enough to drink and nourish your body. This is similar to how *positive thought* works. We add a steady drip of daily positive wisdom into our minds that feed and nourish our souls.

Emile Coue was a French psychologist who developed a method of psychotherapy based on optimistic autosuggestion. He created the mantra: *"Every day, in every way, I'm getting better and better."* Coue taught that by repeating this simple mantra over and over, daily or even hourly, we will experience a new reality. Our life will begin to improve because we're feeding our souls an uplifting message of hope.

There are many ways to feed your soul and nourish your mind. A passage from the Bible, a Buddhist chant, or a beautiful poem or song are just a few examples. But you must become aware of what you're feeding your mind each day. What you feed your mind and soul is just as important as what you feed your body. Fill your body with junk food; you'll get physically sick. Fill your mind with negativity; you'll become mentally sick.

Are you drinking a glass filled with dirty pond water or clean, filtered water? Are you living on a steady diet of negativity and pessimism or positivity and hope? Remind yourself every day, all day long if you have to, that life is good, that you're a good person, that most people are trying to be good, and that all your struggles and efforts are worth it. Develop a healthy habit of positive thoughts and ideas that will sustain you today and bring you hope for tomorrow.

ACTION PLAN

Start each day by repeating the mantra: *"Every day, in every way, I'm getting better and better."*

Repeat it often throughout the day. When you're feeling down, depressed or angry, repeat it. Write it down on a piece of paper and tack it to your bathroom mirror or refrigerator. Keep it close and recite it as often as you need. Find other phrases and mantras that offer positivity and hope, and encourage you to improve and grow continually. Feed your mind and soul positive words, phrases, and ideas until negative thoughts become rare.

SOBERTUDE HABIT #40 — AVOID NEGATIVE MEDIA

The current state of media today is a dark and vicious realm that permeates our lives in the 21st Century. There is a constant storm of negative (and sometimes evil) energy constantly pounding our brains from social media, the daily news, and the entertainment industry.

We live in a time in history when we're bombarded, every hour of every day, by a barrage of negativity, anger, resentment, envy, and division. Turn on the television, and you'll witness a parade of newscasters and pundits screaming about politics and trying their best to divide the country. Go on social media, and you'll be flooded with anger and resentment by a million anonymous trolls, all demanding one thing or another from society (*resentment* seems to be a form of currency on social media). There's an overwhelming amount of anger, hatred, and negativity being spewed forth by fools, pundits, and sociopaths in the media.

The smartest and wisest thing you can do is to avoid or ignore all this media poison. It's almost impossible to avoid it entirely, but you don't have to swim in it every hour, either. Do your best to absorb less social and news media. Instead of watching the news on TV, watch The Comedy Channel or your favorite sitcom. Instead of looking at Facebook for hours, read a book, or take a walk, have lunch with a friend, go fishing, or hit the gym.

We spend so much time these days drowning in negative media, and it's hurting us all. So do yourself a favor and shut off the news pundits and the social media haters. Enjoy your life away from the screens and the screaming. Life is pretty damn good, no matter what all the idiots in the negative media are trying to tell you every second.

ACTION PLAN

Indulging in negative media is a harmful and destructive habit that millions of people struggle with every day. The best way to overcome this soul poison is to turn away from it as often as possible simply. Turn off the news, take a break from social media, stop watching violent movies and television shows. If you can't stop entirely, cut the amount of time in half. Instead of watching two hours of news every night, or spending 2 hours on social media, cut it down to 1 hour. Do whatever it takes to limit the amount of social media that is poisoning all of us.

SOBERTUDE HABIT #41 – HONOR YOUR WORD

Mean what you say, say what you mean.

To be trusted by others, you should always do your best to honor your word, no matter what. Don't say one thing then do something else. Don't say you're going to be somewhere then not show up. Don't promise to complete a project then leave it for someone else to finish. Don't tell someone they can trust you, then turn around and break their trust. Most importantly, don't lie.

Being honest isn't difficult. But we often make it difficult because we're afraid of confronting uncomfortable situations, so we "adjust" the truth or tell "white lies" to avoid confrontation. Being honest and straightforward might ruffle a few feathers occasionally, but ultimately it's better to get the discomfort or confrontation over with quickly. Get it over with now, so you don't have to deal with it later.

Earning people's trust has an enormous impact on friendships, relationships, employment, and marriage. No one wants to put their trust in someone who doesn't honor their word. Once you've been burned by someone a few times, it's only natural to distrust that person and avoid them.

The same rule applies when you deal with someone who never honors their word. If you're lied to by someone close to you, or your trust is being broken repeatedly by someone, it might be best to extract yourself from that relationship. There's no need to spend much time with anyone who consistently lies or breaks promises to you. Move on and surround yourself with people who are honest and trustworthy.

ACTION PLAN

Honoring your word can be summarized and implemented in 4 simple steps:

- Don't lie.

- Don't break promises.

- Keep your commitments.

- Say what you mean, mean what you say.

SOBERTUDE HABIT #42 – PRACTICE COMPASSION

In order to love and be loved, we must nurture a desire and willingness to be compassionate toward all living beings. It's vital that we express empathy for others and always do our best to be helpful to anyone that needs our help.

Practicing compassion and empathy for people who are struggling or less fortunate is a noble goal for everyone to pursue. More compassion in the world would go a long way to reducing strife, violence, conflict, and war.

A central aspect of Buddhism is the development and practice of compassion. Compassion can be practiced in small ways in our daily lives. How do we treat other people? Are we always doing our best to help others? Do we express sympathy when we see someone in pain? Are we charitable with our time, money, or emotions? Do we give more than we take? Are we planting seeds of love in the world instead of adding to the friction?

The key is to see ourselves in others and recognize our shared humanity, realizing we're not much different from each other. We all have anxieties and fears. We all want to be respected and loved. We all need friendship and kindness. Once we start to recognize these simple truths, we're more likely to help others any way we can.

This is true for other beings that inhabit the earth as well. Most animals have a high capacity to feel pain, sadness, and loss. Therefore, we need to recognize their unique spiritual and emotional identity as much as possible, through kindness and respect.

The more compassion you bring to the world, the more you'll receive.

ACTION PLAN

We all face difficulties in life. It's part of being human. But we must try to see ourselves in others and recognize the things that we share as people, not the differences. When others are suffering, we can stop for a moment amidst the chaos of our busy lives and say this simple prayer, before offering our help:

A Prayer of Compassion

There but for the grace of God go I.

May I be kind and compassionate to everyone I meet.

May I be of service to others who need my help.

May I show respect and love towards all beings on earth.

SOBERTUDE HABIT #43 — PRACTICE LOVING-KINDNESS

Is unconditional love possible? Is it a real thing or just a myth? It's easy to point to a mother's devotion to her child as proof that unconditional love exists in the world. But beyond this one example, can we love others without judgment, no matter what? Even people we don't know or people who have hurt us? Is it possible to cultivate compassion and empathy for *everyone*?

Similar to compassion, loving-kindness is unconditional love for everyone and everything. Loving-kindness might be the greatest hope we have of surviving peacefully as a species on earth.

It's not an easy goal to achieve, finding something to love in every person. People hurt each other every day. People can be rude, petty, and spiteful. Human beings can be unpredictable and cruel, capable of horrible acts of violence. Animals, too. Don't believe me? Try kissing a wild grizzly bear on the nose.

Human history abounds with war, genocide, fear, and hate. It's a wonder we survived the 20th Century without blowing up the planet. Seemingly, God's patience with us is limitless. But what we often choose to ignore, and doesn't get much coverage in the media, is that human history is also full of countless stories of kindness and selfless acts of heroism, charity, and deep love.

SOBERTUDE HABIT #43 – PRACTICE LOVING-KINDNESS

One of the best examples of the contrast between love and hate in the human race is the terrorist attacks that occurred on September 11th, 2001, when nineteen religious fanatics blinded by hatred murdered nearly 3,000 people they didn't know. The viciousness and cruelty are unfathomable.

On that same day, however, thousands of firefighters, police officers, and other first responders walked headlong into the inferno to help their fellow citizens. And countless people helped one another in the hours, days, and months that followed this pointless attack. Ultimately, love surpassed hate, as it always does.

Hatred does exist in the human heart. There is no doubt. And we are all capable of tapping into it if we're not careful. But love, the most significant force in the universe, is also a very distinct and deeply-rooted aspect of our humanity.

To cultivate love, compassion, and forgiveness, even for those who wish to harm us, is the most critical thing we can strive for in our lifetime on earth.

We must find a way to forgive others (and ourselves) of any misdeeds, and attempt always to find the best in everyone. We must understand that many people are so blinded by fear, ignorance, and sadness that they lash out at others with cruel and often violent acts.

If we encounter a stray dog, do we hate the dog if it bites us? Or do we understand that the dog is probably reacting out of fear and ignorance of our intention? The dog is only doing what he thinks he must do to survive. There is no point in hating or resenting the dog. Instead, we should cultivate compassion and understanding for it...*and then go to the doctor for a rabies shot.*

This isn't to suggest that people who hurt others should go unpunished. In many cases, they should—but we must rely on the rule of law, especially when violence or murder is involved. But it's crucial

117

to start practicing loving-kindness towards everyone and everything. Otherwise, we will suffocate on our resentment, fear, and hatred, and the cycle will continue endlessly.

ACTION PLAN

Practicing loving-kindness is about releasing judgment, even under the worst conditions. Find a way to open your heart to EVERY being on earth, without judgment or resentment. Try always to remember that the kinder you are to others, the kinder they will be toward you.

SOBERTUDE HABIT #44 – COMPLIMENT OTHERS

One of the kindest things you can do each day is to pay someone a simple compliment. This doesn't mean fawning over people or being obsequious. It simply means that when you notice an appealing quality about another person, whether a friend or stranger, you make a positive comment designed to make them feel good.

We all enjoy hearing compliments about ourselves, especially when we're unhappy or depressed. It can make a huge difference in how we feel for the rest of the day. Extending that same positive energy towards other people can be as simple as saying a few kind words that make them smile or lifts their mood.

There are countless things to look for if you want to compliment someone: something they're wearing; something they say; their sense of humor; the type of work they do; a distinct physical attribute. This last one, a distinct physical attribute, requires a great deal of caution. Paying someone a compliment about their physical appearance, especially towards a stranger or someone of the opposite sex, is fraught with danger. Don't compliment someone's body or face unless you know it won't feel inappropriate or threatening.

Compliments make people feel good. They can also make you feel better about yourself, knowing that you brightened up someone's life. Compliments help bring people closer together, as well.

Once you set your mind to complimenting others, you'll be encouraged to start looking for the best in people. You'll begin to see good things about others that maybe you once missed or ignored. This is a great way to become less self-centered and to practice loving-kindness everywhere you go.

Compliments often have a ripple effect, too. When you compliment someone, that person is more likely to do the same thing for someone else. Thus, the positive energy you started ripples outward into the world like a pebble dropped into a pond.

Reasons to compliment other people:

- **Makes them feel good about themselves**
- **Encourages you to see the best in others**
- **Brings people closer together**
- **Makes social interaction more comfortable**
- **Decreases tension and distrust between people**
- **Creates positive energy between people**
- **Creates a positive ripple effect in the world**

Make it a point to pay more compliments to people each day. Not only will you make others feel better, but you'll also feel better as well.

ACTION PLAN

- **Be on the lookout for interesting or positive things about other people.**
- **Make it a habit to compliment at least one person every day.**

- Avoid complimenting people on their physical appearance unless you know for sure it's appropriate or non-threatening.

- Don't embarrass people by over-complimenting them.

- Keep each compliment short, sweet, and straightforward.

SOBERTUDE HABIT #45 — INSPIRE PEOPLE

We all need a little encouragement from time to time. There are moments when we all want or need someone to tell us we're doing a good job and that our efforts matter. We all want to be recognized for the things that we do well and to have others appreciate whatever skills or talents we possess. Inspiring others to be and do their best is one of the most positive contributions you can make to the world.

Similar to complimenting others, inspiring people forces you to look for the best in everyone. Once you can identify the gifts and talents that other people possess, it becomes easier to encourage them.

Always look for ways to build people up so that they feel good about themselves. The better they feel, the more they will be able to achieve in life.

You probably know what it feels like when someone recognizes a quality about you and expresses their admiration. We all have those special moments when someone inspired us to pursue a particular talent because they saw that we had potential or a gift. Those compliments and words of encouragement can last a lifetime, filling us with enthusiasm and confidence every time we experience self-doubt or discouragement.

If you notice someone with a particular type of skill or do something out of the ordinary that seems unique or truly interesting, let them know. Share your admiration. By sharing your enthusiasm, you can light the fire within their soul that pushes them to excel.

Celebrate the accomplishments of other people as often as you can. Don't allow yourself to drown in envy and jealousy, two highly destructive personality traits. Instead, take joy in seeing another person achieve or exhibit something good or wonderful.

Encourage others to achieve more in life by expressing whatever you admire about them. Everyone has something admirable within them that makes them unique. Everyone! There's not a single person alive who doesn't possess a particular talent or interesting quality. Look for those talents and qualities in others, and inspire them by pointing them out and expressing your admiration.

ACTION PLAN

Be on the lookout for what makes other people special and unique. When you spot something that stands out, pay them a compliment and encourage them to grow in that quality. Push people, gently, to pursue whatever they desire to achieve, especially if they show a particular talent or skill in that area. Find the best in people and inspire them to achieve greater things in life.

SOBERTUDE HABIT #46 — DEVELOP OPTIMISM

Do you see the glass half empty or half full? Do you see the world through cynical, pessimistic eyes or positive, optimistic eyes?

According to the Mayo Clinic, positive thinking helps with stress management, improves your health, and can increase your life span. The simple fact is that if you cultivate a positive, optimistic attitude, you might live longer. But even if you don't live longer, your life will be more joyful with less anxiety, stress, and fear. To quote Norman Vincent Peale: *"Change your thoughts, and you can change your world."*

Optimism is defined as hopefulness and confidence about the future or the successful outcome of something. Being optimistic only requires small adjustments in how you think.

Train yourself to look at the future with hope and anticipation and discard irrational fears that tell you everything sucks and will turn out badly.

Optimism has many proven benefits, including:

- Lowers distress
- Reduces fear
- Reduces anxiety

- Reduces depression
- Improves cardiovascular health
- Improves overall physical health
- Increased life span
- Improves social interaction
- Improves friendships and family relationships

You don't have to be a genius to realize that upbeat, optimistic people are more pleasant and enjoyable and generally have more friends. As we've discussed, many people are unable or unwilling to let go of resentment and anger. *Woe-is-me-ism* is a real and far too common mental ailment that plagues many people. The idea that they've been dealt a bad hand in life often leaves people feeling pessimistic about the future. Negativity and pessimism get you nowhere and just adds to anger, sadness, and depression.

Like your spiritual health, your mental health has a significant impact on your life. Develop an optimistic outlook for the future. Strive for a positive view of every part of your life. **Embrace optimism as your new reality** by deciding that the glass is half full not half empty

ACTION PLAN

It's crucial to develop an optimistic attitude by changing your thinking. Whenever you feel fear or anxiety rising about what will happen in the future, write it down, then <u>counteract your negative thoughts with a positive, hopeful prediction</u>:

- **Today I'm feeling fearful about the following issue (Example:** *I will lose my job***):**

- **Counteract your fear with a favorable forecast (Example: *If I lose my job, I will pick myself up and find a better job*):**

You can apply this technique to any part of life. Whenever you feel anxious about an issue, simply replace your negative thinking with an optimistic counter-reaction that is hopeful and positive.

SOBERTUDE HABIT #47 — CHERISH YOUR PARTNER

If you're married, in a committed relationship, or hope to be in a future relationship, cherish your partner and show them genuine respect and love. Never take for granted that someone is sharing all, or a significant part of their life with you.

Your primary interest in the relationship should be to foster their personal development as a human being. Always be available to provide him or her with the moral, spiritual, and emotional support they need under every circumstance. As we've stated before, give more that you take.

Being in a relationship with someone requires loyalty and a great deal of devotion to that person's happiness. When we're very young and first start dating, we tend to be selfish in our pursuits – *what's in it for me?* But the sign of a truly healthy relationship is an equal give-and-take between partners where both people are sharing the responsibilities for each other's well-being, peace, and growth.

If your aim in a relationship is purely self-focused (feeding your ego, sexual gratification, financial gain, etc.), then the relationship is probably doomed from the start. Cultivating a deep sense of moral responsibility for another person is one of the most satisfying and enriching experiences you can ever experience. Every healthy relationship requires empathy, tenderness, and respect for the other person's feelings, ambitions, and desires.

Instead of seeing your partner as a competitor, see them as a friend. Rather than thinking about what your partner can do for you, look for ways to bring them joy. Instead of always looking to receive love, give love.

But it also has to work both ways to succeed. Your partner needs to cherish and *respect you in return.* You don't want to be the only one who is giving. You don't want to be a doormat in the relationship. Your relationship with your partner needs to be rooted in trust, devotion, loyalty, and kindness; otherwise, the road ahead is going to be bumpy and probably heartbreaking.

ACTION PLAN

There are numerous ways to grow and improve your relationship with your partner (and many good books on the topic). Your top 6 relationship habits should include:

- Communicate openly and honestly with each other.

- Respect each other's points of view on every topic (especially when you disagree).

- Encourage your partner's growth and development.

- Provide them with emotional, spiritual, and moral support.

- Compliment them honestly and often.

- Tell them you love them or care about them (as often as possible).

SOBERTUDE HABIT #48 — DEVELOP EMPATHY

One of the unique gifts humans possess is the ability to feel what other people are feeling. Most people can sense what another person is feeling during times of stress, fear, anger, sadness, and joy.

One reason movies are so popular is that we can experience the extreme emotions of the characters in the film; we're able to connect and empathize with their emotional experience within the relative safety of the movie theater or our living room. The same thing is true with certain types of songs; we're able to feel what the singer is expressing through the lyrics, connecting and empathizing with the character's emotions.

Empathy is the ability to understand and share the feelings of another person. Have you ever had someone offer you kindness and comfort when you were in pain? Has anyone ever teared up for you when someone you loved died? Has a friend ever comforted you through heartbreak?

Our ability to connect with one another and feel what the other person is experiencing is the root cause of kindness and love. The more empathy we have, the more compassion and love we're able to offer others.

It's often the kindness and empathy that we receive from another person that saves us from falling into the emotional abyss.

A sympathetic word, a comforting hug, or a heartfelt conversation can make the difference between devastation and recovery.

For many of us, empathy is something that has to be developed and practiced. It's easy to become caught up in our selfish pursuits, blinded by our ambitions and desires. When we allow ourselves to become too absorbed in our lives, we miss opportunities to feel and experience what people are experiencing.

One of the most enriching and fulfilling things you can do is to help others in their time of need. By keeping yourself aware of what other people are experiencing, especially those close to you, you will be able to offer them the emotional support, kindness, and love they might need to survive any pain or heartbreak that befalls them.

Keep yourself attuned to what the people around you are feeling. Be aware of the emotional upset or pain that they might be experiencing. You might have a huge impact on their lives by offering a sympathetic ear or a few kind words, saving them from slipping too deeply into more suffering.

Empathy can also be a way to share in their joy and accomplishments. It isn't only about to recognize and reacting to the pain of other people. You can also celebrate the victories and happiness that other people are feeling through encouragement and compliments.

ACTION PLAN

By training yourself to become more mindful of what other people are feeling, you will have more opportunities to help or encourage them whenever they experience extreme emotions, both good and bad. When you recognize any form of pain or suffering by someone, decide if its a proper time to step in and offer your friendship, advice, comforting words, or just a good old fashioned hug. Be careful not to overstep your bounds or be intrusive. Sometimes people prefer to be left alone in their pain or grief).

SOBERTUDE HABIT #49 – BECOME A BETTER LISTENER

Being a good listener is something that everyone cherishes in another person. We all want to be heard and have our feelings recognized and understood, especially by the people we love. Being a good, attentive listener is our opportunity to show other people that we care for them and are concerned with their life experience as much as our own.

However, the problem is that many of us find it difficult to concentrate on what anyone is saying because of the cacophony of noise in our own heads. We can become so overloaded with our thoughts that it's easy to tune out everyone else. Or we try to offer advice when sometimes it's more helpful and appropriate to simply *say nothing* and just listen to what the other person has to say.

Listening is a skill that can be developed by most people. Very few people are naturally good listeners. Most of us need to focus our attention on what other people are saying, or our minds will quickly drift off to other things like our shopping lists, the kid's homework, paying bills, or any of the millions that we have to deal with every day. To become a good listener:

- Take a genuine interest in what the other person has to say.

- Avoid interrupting them for as long as possible.

- If you begin to drift off, catch yourself, and bring your focus back on them.

- Allow them to dominate the conversation without you taking it over.

- Avoid offering your opinion unless they ask for it.

- Ask open-ended questions without expecting any specific answer.

- Empathize with their feelings and emotions as they speak

Becoming a good listener isn't always easy, but it's a necessary and helpful skill to develop. Most importantly, being a good listener is an excellent opportunity to be of service to someone else who might need a sympathetic ear to work through their pain, sadness, frustration, or confusion.

We all want to be listened to when we speak. The better we listen to others, the more likely they'll return the favor someday when we need it the most.

ACTION PLAN

Listening to other people often requires concentration and focus. Pay attention to what other people are saying, especially when they're in pain. Keep your mind on their thoughts and words, free from judgment. Remain quiet as long as possible. Use each opportunity as a way to learn something about them and to share (empathize) in their plight as if it were your own experience.

SOBERTUDE HABIT #50 — SMILE MORE OFTEN

There are times when the clothes we wear affect how we feel. When we walk into a room wearing our favorite shirt or blouse, we'll automatically express confidence without even trying. There's just something about wearing certain clothes that makes us feel good about ourselves and the image we project to the world.

Wearing a smile can also boost your confidence and change how you feel. Likewise, it can cheer up everyone around you.

Make it a choice to smile more often. It's that simple. You don't have to smile big with your teeth exposed while you're walking around outside. If you do that, you'll just feel weird and frighten people. Instead, make it a point to smile gently throughout your day, no matter what is happening.

It's especially helpful to start your morning with a gentle smile. If you start your day in a dark, angry mood (frowning), you will often remain that way during the entire experience. But if you begin your day with a smile, your mood will quickly become more positive.

Let's face it; some days we just feel like crap. We wake up in a bad mood or have to face some difficulty that makes us anxious or depressed. Instead of giving in to these dark moods, if we can smile, it sometimes has a significant impact on our attitude and outlook.

Scientific studies show that smiling releases dopamine, endorphins, and serotonin into our brains. These are our feel-good neurotransmitters (also known as "happy chemicals"). These transmitters have an immediate impact on one's mood and state of well-being. At the same time, smiling decreases stress hormones and lowers blood pressure. Smiling also sends a signal to the world that we're not a threat. It can relieve tension for ourselves and those around us.

A well-timed smile throughout the day can go a long way to altering your mood and the mood of those around you.

Offer the world a smile.

ACTION PLAN

- Smile more.
- Smile often.
- Choose to be happy.

FINAL THOUGHTS

What's the point of all these habits and exercises? Why should you even bother with paying attention to any of the things we've covered in this book?

Happiness and gratitude are both choices. We must CHOOSE to be happy. We must CHOOSE to be grateful. Often happiness and gratitude, like all good things in life, require effort and work.

The habits that we've discussed in this book can be implemented in your life today and every day, if you're willing to try. With a small amount of effort, developing healthy, positive habits will lead you down a path of optimism and hope. You will find that life becomes a little easier and that you're open to new things and are more joyful and content.

This will be a great benefit to your health and emotional well-being. It will also make other people around you happier when they see how your life is changing and improving.

The most important thing you can do for yourself and the people you love is to develop an attitude-of-gratitude in every part of your life. Practice these simple habits every day, or whenever you can. Share them with other people. Work daily on your outlook on life and stay optimistic about your future.

The difference between a sad life and a happy life is the attitude we choose to carry. I hope this will be a new beginning for your life in gratitude, abundance, joy, and peace.

SOBERTUDE

I wish you and your loved ones well.

###

CAN I GET YOUR HELP?

As an independent author, I rely on reader feedback to generate awareness of my books. If you have time, I would truly appreciate your honest opinion of this book on Amazon or wherever you bought it, or social media, so other people can benefit from your opinion.

Thank you and many blessings.

Dirk Foster

Connect With Me:

Join My Newsletter and Receive a FREE BOOK at: ***www.thesober-journey.com***
Facebook: ***www.facebook.com/sobertravels/***
Author Page: ***https://www.facebook.com/Dirk-Foster-Author-105017227522728/?modal=admin_todo_tour***

Other Books by Dirk Foster:

 **Polluted:
My Sober Journey:
Alcohol, Addiction
and The 7 Stages to
Getting Clean**

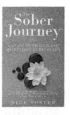 **The Sober Journey:
A Guide to Prayer
and Meditation
in Recovery**

 **Sober Body:
A Guide to Health
and Fitness
in Sobriety**

 **Sober and Broke:
How to Make
Money, Save
Money, Pay Debt
and Find Financial
Peace is Sobriety**

Printed in Great Britain
by Amazon

17707446R00079